JOHN OF SALISBURY

MEDIEVAL AND RENAISSANCE
TEXTS AND STUDIES

VOLUME 288

JOHN OF SALISBURY

By
Cary J. Nederman

Arizona Center for Medieval and Renaissance Studies
Tempe, Arizona
2005

Library of Congress Cataloging-in-Publication Data

Nederman, Cary J.
  John of Salisbury / by Cary J. Nederman.
    p. cm. — (Medieval and Renaissance Texts and Studies ; v. 288)
  Includes bibliographical references and index.
  ISBN-13: 978-0-86698-331-0 (alk. paper)
  ISBN-10: 0-86698-331-7 (alk. paper)
  1. John, of Salisbury, Bishop of Chartres, d. 1180. 2. Philosophers,
Medieval—Biography.   I. Title. II. Series: Medieval & Renaissance
Texts & Studies (Series) ; v. 288.

  B765.J44N43 2005
  189'.4—dc22
  [B]

                                            2005020440

This book is made to last.
It is set in Hiroshige Std Book
and printed on acid-free paper
to library specifications.

Printed in the United States of America

Cover Image:
Charles V dans sa librairie, from
Bibliothèque nationale de France (Manuscripts Department,
Western Section, Fr. 24287, fol. 2) Denis Foulechat,
Translation of John of Salisbury's *Policraticus*, Paris, 14th century,

For Constant J. Mews and John O. Ward

TABLE OF CONTENTS

ACKNOWLEDGEMENTS

My introduction to John of Salisbury occurred nearly a quarter-century ago at the instigation of my doctoral supervisor, the late John Brückmann, with whom I jointly authored my first published essay on the topic. Although I have worked on John's thought sporadically over the years, it has never been too far from my mind that I would eventually produce a general survey of his life and writings. That I do so now is the result of several happy coincidences. In 1997, while still a member of the faculty of the University of Arizona, I was asked to give a course of lectures on England in the age of John of Salisbury to a summer program at St. Catharine's College, Cambridge, sponsored by the Arizona Center for Medieval and Renaissance Studies. Preparation of the notes for this lecture series—entitled " 'The Shoulders of Giants': Twelfth-Century England through the Eyes of John of Salisbury"—afforded the opportunity to draft a rough outline of the present book. This outline still contained as many questions as answers. Thanks are due to students and colleagues in July and August of 1997, who provided such a stimulating environment for me to "think aloud" about the details as well as the broad contours of John's career.

Coincidentally, John Smedley, of Variorum, which published a series entitled "Authors of the Middle Ages," invited me to submit a proposal to him for a short volume on John of Salisbury. In the interim, plans were made for the series to be acquired by Medieval and Renaissance Texts and Studies, a branch of the Arizona Center, and Dr. Smedley permitted me to transfer my proposal to the General Editor of MRTS, Professor Robert Bjork. I must thank both individuals for their support of this enterprise and their cooperation in making it a reality.

Several of my earlier articles concerning John of Salisbury were co-authored with former students who greatly aided me in appreciating elements of his thinking that I had overlooked. I would be remiss not to credit these collaborators by name: Catherine Campbell, Arlen Feldwick, Elaine Lawson, and Jacqui True. Kate Langdon Forhan's love of John and her friendship have been sources of continual encouragement to me through two decades. Christopher Crockett has supplied me with references, ideas, and moral support, gently drawing my attention to my gaps in knowledge about the minutiae of John's later life. Donnalee Dox read the manuscript in its entirety and saved me, as always, from numerous egregious errors. Marcia Colish and an anonymous reader for MRTS made numerous invaluable suggestions for improving the book. Sabina Flanagan and Constant Mews provided important information at crucial moments. My colleagues in political science at Texas A&M University—especially Edward Portis and Elisabeth Ellis—eased the process of composition of the book in myriad ways. Dr. Leslie MacCoull once again copyedited the manuscript with enthusiasm and precision. A Faculty Fellowship from the Texas A&M Center for Humanities Research aided final revision of manuscript.

Australia has generated a remarkable flow of scholarship on the twelfth century during the past several decades, and many of my most intensive periods of
thinking about John of Salisbury in relation to his times have resulted from my
contact with denizens of that often overlooked continent. This volume is dedicated to two people who have played an especially pivotal role in guiding my
understanding of John and the multiple facets of his intellectual and literary
achievements: Constant J. Mews of Monash University and John O. Ward of the
University of Sydney. Without their inspiration and model scholarship to spur
me on, this little book would have failed utterly to hit its target.

College Station, Texas
July 2002

ABBREVIATIONS

CCCM = Corpus Christianorum Continuatio Medievalis

Keats-Rohan = John of Salisbury, *Policraticus I–IV*, ed. K. S. B. Keats-Rohan, CCCM 118 (Turnhout: Brepols, 1993)

MB = *Materials for the History of Thomas Becket, Archbishop of Canterbury*, ed. J. C. Robertson and J. B. Shepard, 7 vols. (London: Rolls Series, 1875–1885)

PL = *Patrologiae cursus completus, series Latina*, ed. J. P. Migne

Webb = John of Salisbury, *Policraticus*, ed. Clement C. J. Webb, 2 vols. (Oxford: Clarendon Press, 1909)

WJS = *The World of John of Salisbury*, ed. Michael Wilks (Oxford: Basil Blackwell, 1984)

CHAPTER ONE

LIFE AND CAREER

John of Salisbury has earned a considerable and well-deserved reputation as an original thinker as well as an observant witness to the vast intellectual and cultural changes that engulfed twelfth-century Europe. John's varied career virtually defies classification. Educated in France by nearly all the best minds of his time and in a comprehensive course of study, he turned to public affairs in the service of the English church, becoming an intimate of archbishops, popes, and kings. Yet amidst his political entanglements, he still found time to compose two of the most important and influential philosophical works of the mid-twelfth century—the *Policraticus* and the *Metalogicon*—along with a number of other writings in various genres. John survived the ordeal of the conflict between Archbishop of Canterbury Thomas Becket and King Henry II, and devoted his last years to chronicling the turbulent times he had experienced. Late in life, he was himself raised to high ecclesiastical office as bishop of Chartres.

John's remarkable life and writings have stimulated a large body of scholarship that has expanded noticeably during the past half-century, altering and deepening our appreciation of the nature and significance of his contributions to twelfth-century intellectual life. We now possess a far more complete understanding of his source materials, his intended audience, his relationships with academic and political friends and foes, and the processes and methods he employed in composing his texts. Yet the substantial progress in scholarship on John has not up to the present generated a new biobibliographical study of him. The last comprehensive examination of John's life and intellectual activity, by Hans Liebeschütz, was published in 1950.[1] The proceedings of the 1980 commemorative conference held at Salisbury are extremely useful but too fragmentary to present a clear overview of the current state of scholarship on John.[2] The present volume proposes to distill and crystallize the recent advances in the appraisal of John's career and thought.

---

[1] Hans Liebeschütz, *Mediaeval Humanism in the Life and Writings of John of Salisbury* (London: The Warburg Institute, 1950). The volume was reprinted with an epilogue appended in 1968. Klaus Guth provides a very useful and thorough survey of John's life and circle of associates—but not an evaluation of his teachings—in *Johannes von Salisbury (1115/20–1180): Studien zur Kirchen-, Kultur- und Sozialgeschichte Westeuropas im 12. Jahrhundert* (St. Ottilien: Eos Verlag, 1978). Gabriella Zanoletti's *Il bello come vero alla Scuola di Chartres: Giovanni di Salisbury* (Rome: Luciano Lucanini Editore, 1979) is a brief and superficial overview that lacks awareness of some of the important literature from the 1960s and 1970s in German and English on John and his context.

[2] These were published as *WJS*.

At the same time, there remain many issues about John that stand in need of resolution. Among the outstanding questions that demand attention are:

1. When precisely did John write his major works? The long-standing supposition that he engaged in a flurry of literary activity in the late 1150s—at a time when, by his own admission, he was also overwhelmed with administrative duties—has become increasingly implausible.

2. What were John's true attitudes toward his teachers as well as the various classical and contemporary schools of thought to which he was exposed? His criticisms of contemporary intellectual trends, which were often veiled in pseudonyms, require further examination, especially in light of the prosecution of several of his teachers by ecclesiastical tribunals for holding allegedly unorthodox doctrines.

3. Was John in fact the friend and intimate of Thomas Becket that has often been assumed? An unbiased reading of the textual evidence raises serious doubts that John was a member of Becket's inner circle.

4. How did John's career proceed after the murder of Becket? There has been decidedly little study of the final decade of his life, in particular, his work on behalf of Becket's canonization and his years as bishop of Chartres.

5. What relationship exists between John's contributions as a major intellectual figure and his activities in the world of ecclesiastical and secular politics? The tendency to isolate these two elements of his life, and to treat John-as-author separately from John-as-churchman, appears untenable in the light of many declarations about himself found in his writings.

An aim of this volume will be to make an original contribution to scholarship by seeking resolution—if only provisionally—of these and other lingering dilemmas raised by John of Salisbury's career.

Early Life and Education (1115/1120–1147)

John of Salisbury has been burdened with a misnomer. He was actually born and raised not in modern Salisbury, but in what is now called Old Sarum (the original hilltop site of Salisbury). The standard dating of his birth to between 1115 and 1120 is estimated by counting backward from the known facts of his later life. Evidence of his family background is scant.[3] About his parents, we know only of his mother's long illness from a letter of 1170.[4] His younger brother, Richard, was a canon (at Exeter and then Merton) and also a partisan in the

---

[3] The best recent analysis is Frank Barlow, "John of Salisbury and His Brothers," *Journal of Ecclesiastical History* 46 (1995): 95–109.

[4] John of Salisbury, *The Letters of John of Salisbury*, v. 2, ed. W. J. Millor and C. N. L. Brooke (hereafter *Letters,* 2) (Oxford: Clarendon Press, 1979): 716–17 (Letter 304).

Becket controversy. Richard joined his brother in exile on the continent during the 1160s, and several of John's letters to him are extant.[5] An older half-brother, Robert, a canon of Exeter and later archdeacon of Totnes, is also a recipient of John's correspondence.[6] We encounter passing mention of a kinsman named Richard—not John's brother—who was a student of Master Gerard Pucelle[7] and who died in 1168; he may have been the son of Master Geoffrey of St. Edmund, whose relation to John is unknown.[8]

Whether John was from noble blood is uncertain. He remarks in a letter from the 1160s that he is "a man small in name (*hominem Parvum nomine*)," which may be a pun on a nickname ("John the Runt") or on a family name ("John Little"); or again it may indicate that he does not hail from a lineage of "good name."[9] He does not in any case seem to have possessed significant means; he says that he taught the sons of the nobility in Paris in order to support his own studies, and in later years he repeatedly complains of his financial burdens and penury.[10] Eventually, he seems to have ended his education for lack of income. In later years, John frets about being deprived of revenue from churches bestowed upon him through his service to Canterbury.[11]

Despite John's longstanding association with successive archbishops of Canterbury in his maturity, he almost certainly did not study at its cathedral school. This is suggested by the fact that he required a letter of introduction (from Bernard of Clairvaux) to Archbishop Theobald when he came to work at Canterbury upon the completion of his education. It is likely, rather, that John's earliest ("grammar") schooling occurred at Old Sarum, a cathedral whose educational facilities dated to the late eleventh century.[12] John's more advanced ("higher") studies probably occurred at Exeter, since both he and his brother maintained an established connection with that cathedral well into the 1170s. Moreover, many of John's close friends and associates also fell within the ambit of Exeter. The cathedral school at Exeter was larger and more cosmopolitan than Old Sarum in its student body as well as its faculty. In addition to both primary and secondary education, Exeter offered at least rudimentary instruction in

---

[5] *Letters*, 2:84–87 (Letter 164), 118–19 (Letter 169), 128–33 (Letter 172), 576–77 (Letter 279), 716–17 (Letter 304), 722–23 (Letter 304).

[6] *Letters*, 2:36–47 (Letters 145–148).

[7] See Yoko Hirata, "John of Salisbury, Gerard Pucelle and *amicitia*," in *Friendship in Medieval Europe*, ed. Julian Haseldine (Stroud: Sutton, 1999), 153–65.

[8] *Letters*, 2:76–77 (Letter 161), 594–95 (Letter 277).

[9] *Letters*, 2:342–43 (Letter 212). Some biographers have taken this "small" reference as license to suggest that he was weak of constitution, finding evidence in a remark in the *Policraticus* about physicians; see Beryl Smalley, *The Becket Conflict and the Schools* (Oxford: Basil Blackwell, 1973), 87. This seems to strain credulity.

[10] John of Salisbury, *Metalogicon*, ed. J. B. Hall and K. S. B. Keats-Rohan, CCCM 98 (Turnhout: Brepols, 1991), 72.

[11] E.g., *Letters*, 2:716–17 (Letter 304).

[12] Nicholas Orme, *Education in the West of England 1066–1548* (Exeter: University of Exeter Press, 1976), 65–66; for a useful description of the provincial cathedral schools, see 1–26.

theology and canon law, whereas that does not seem to have been the case at Old Sarum during John's time.[13]

The only other information we possess about John's early life comes from his own account in the *Policraticus* of a brush with the occult arts.[14] Having been placed as a boy in the charge of a priest in order to receive instruction in the Psalter, John narrates his initiation (along with an older youth) into crystal-gazing and necromancy by his teacher. Apparently John had no aptitude for perceiving spirits, for he was soon excluded from the proceedings, for which he expresses extreme gratitude, since all of those who engaged in such practices were thereafter afflicted with miseries of the flesh. Even the priest, who subsequently renounced magic and became a canon, suffered for his prior misdeeds. Whether this story refers to events in his native Old Sarum, or to occurrences elsewhere (probably Exeter), is unclear, but the former seems the likelier.[15]

The earliest firm date that we can associate with John is 1136 (identified by him as the year following the death of King Henry I), when, by his own recounting in a famous autobiographical passage of the *Metalogicon*, he traveled to Paris to undertake advanced studies. The structure of a twelfth-century "higher" education was built around the seven liberal arts, which were divided into the basic subjects of the *trivium* (grammar, rhetoric, and dialectic) and the advanced topics of the *quadrivium* (arithmetic, music, geometry, and astronomy). While generally speaking the former were regarded as preparatory to the latter, there was no overarching sequence in which the fields of knowledge had to be studied, as the example of John's own learning will illustrate. However, it was expected that a student would have fairly complete mastery of the liberal arts prior to undertaking the investigation of theology, "the queen of the sciences."

John's narration of his twelve years of education has formed an important source for the understanding of French higher instruction in the twelfth century. For much of the last one hundred and fifty years, the *Metalogicon* was taken as definitive evidence for the existence of a major (even preeminent) center of intellectual activity at Chartres.[16] It was understood to describe a sequence of events involving an initial period of study at Paris, then a departure to Chartres, and an eventual return to Paris. Only in the last few years has the "School of Chartres" thesis been debunked, first by Sir Richard Southern's careful reconstruction of

---

[13] Orme, *Education in the West of England*, 42–43, 45–53.

[14] Keats-Rohan, 167–68.

[15] David Rollo has connected this episode with the courtiers' magical practices decried in the *Policraticus*; see *Glamorous Sorcery: Magic and Literacy in the High Middle Ages* (Minneapolis: University of Minnesota Press, 2000), 32–56.

[16] A brief summary of the history of the "School of Chartres" controversy is offered by K. S. B. Keats-Rohan, "John of Salisbury and Education in Twelfth-Century Paris from the Account of His *Metalogicon*," *History of Universities* 6 (1986): 1–45, here 8–9. A last-ditch, and not especially compelling, attempt to defend the existence of the "School of Chartres" has been produced by Édouard Jeauneau, *L'âge d'or des Écoles de Chartres*, rev. ed. (Chartres: Éditions Houvet, 2000).

the evidence,[17] and more recently by the replacement of Webb's very poor edition of the *Metalogicon* with a much more reliable text, edited by J. B. Hall and Katherine Keats-Rohan.[18] It now seems clear that all of the instruction received by John between 1136 and 1147 occurred in Paris and its environs, and that the author of the *Metalogicon* did not witness any great moment of intellectual vigor at Chartres.

Keats-Rohan is correct to point out that the autobiographical narrative of the *Metalogicon* is ultimately inseparable from John's philosophical motive for its inclusion, namely, to highlight the dangers of a narrow education in dialectic.[19] But we may still extract a useful set of facts about John's activities in Paris.[20] In 1136, John commenced instruction at Mont-Ste.-Geneviève under the famed and controversial teacher Peter Abelard ("*Peripateticus Palatinus*"). Charismatic as well as brilliant, Abelard attracted to his lectures a large audience; indeed, it may have been Abelard's wide reputation for intellectual prowess that initially drew John to Paris. From Abelard, John reports learning the "first principles" of the art of dialectic, hanging on the words of the Master with unconcealed enthusiasm. When Abelard ceased to teach at Paris the following year, John expressed dismay that his mentor had departed too soon.[21]

Scholars have generally not viewed John as a follower of Abelard, a position justified by the sharp divergence between the two regarding the status of universals (Abelard adopting a nominalist position, according to which universal terms are "words").[22] Yet in the *Metalogicon* as well as in the earlier *Entheticus*

---

[17] The original statement of this position is to be found in R. W. Southern, "Humanism and the School of Chartres," in idem, *Medieval Humanism and Other Studies* (Oxford: Basil Blackwell, 1970), 61–85. The argument was reiterated and defended by Southern prior to his death in *Scholastic Humanism and the Unification of Europe*, 1, *Foundations* (Oxford: Blackwell, 1995), 58–101. Of course, Southern has not been without his revisers and critics. Two of the most recent interesting respondents are Winthrop Wetherbee, "Philosophy, Cosmology, and the Twelfth-Century Renaissance," in *A History of Twelfth-Century Philosophy*, ed. Peter Dronke (Cambridge: Cambridge University Press, 1988), 21–53 and John Marenbon, "Humanism, Scholasticism and the School of Chartres," *International Journal of the Classical Tradition* 6 (2000): 569–77.

[18] For criticism and correction of the serious blunders in Webb's edition, see J. B. Hall, "Toward a Text of John of Salisbury's 'Metalogicon'," *Studi Medievali* 3rd ser. 24 (1983): 791–816 and especially K. S. B. Keats-Rohan, "The Textual Tradition of John of Salisbury's *Metalogicon*," *Revue d'histoire des textes* 16 (1986): 229–82.

[19] Keats-Rohan, "John of Salisbury and Education in Twelfth-Century Paris," 20.

[20] The following chronological sequence is based on K. S. B. Keats-Rohan, "The Chronology of John of Salisbury's Studies in France: A Reading of 'Metalogicon' II.10," *Studi Medievali* 3rd ser. 28 (1987): 193–203. See also Southern, *Scholastic Humanism and the Unification of Europe*, 1:214–21. An extremely useful brief survey of the figures with whom John studied is Constant Mews, "Philosophy and Theology 1100–1150: The Search for Harmony," in *Le XIIe Siècle: Mutations et renouveau en France dans la première moitié du XIIe siècle*, ed. Françoise Gasparri (Paris: Le Léopard d'Or, 1995), 159–203.

[21] *Metalogicon*, 70–71.

[22] *Metalogicon*, 81. Also Webb 2:142. Various alternative terms to "nominalism"

de Dogmate Philosophorum and the later *Historia Pontificalis*, John expresses his friendship and admiration for Abelard and his devotees.[23] The *Metalogicon* praises Abelard as a teacher "who won such distinction in logic among all his contemporaries that it was thought that he alone really understood Aristotle."[24] The very appellation *Peripateticus Palatinus* that John employs repeatedly reinforces a connection between the "original" and the "latter-day" Aristotle, a very great honorific indeed. Even when John explicitly disputes Abelard's teachings about universals, which he clearly regards to be misguided, he still claims that those who subscribe to Abelardian principles "are my friends," in spite of their obstinate insistence upon the correctness of their views.[25] Among John's teachers and associates in Paris, only the theologian Gilbert of Poitiers receives as generally sympathetic a treatment in the *Metalogicon* as Abelard. (Is it any coincidence, one wonders, that these two favored figures in John's intellectual life were also both prosecuted before church councils for their doctrines by no less vaunted a personage than Bernard of Clairvaux?) While John's noted intellectual eclecticism would surely prevent him from self-identification as the member of any "school" or "sect" (except perhaps the Ciceronian New Academy, with its moderate skepticism and probabilism), serious investigation remains to be devoted to evaluation of philosophical debts that might be owed to Abelard.[26] At minimum, John sees no reason to conceal his admiration for a twice-condemned heretic and his "friendship" toward the followers of such a person. And John heaps praise upon Abelard for his modest recognition of a profound debt to the past for making possible his own thought, whereas so many contemporaries lacked awareness of authorities and thus claimed credit for the invention of ideas that had long been proposed.[27]

(such as "conceptualism" or "non-realism") have been proposed to describe Abelard's position. As Constant Mews has pointed out to me in a private correspondence, however, "nominalism" has some historical claim to be an accurate term: Abelard was perceived as a nominalist in logic by his contemporaries and his students in logic were known as *nominales*. On this vexed problem, also see Martin M. Tweedale, "Logic: From the Late Eleventh Century to the Time of Abelard," in *A History of Twelfth-Century Philosophy*, ed. Dronke, 219–21; Y. Iwakuma, "Twelfth-Century Nominales: The Posthumous School of Peter Abelard," *Vivarium* 30 (1992): 97–109; and idem, " 'Vocales,' or Early Nominalists," *Traditio* 47 (1992): 37–111.

[23] The relevant passages of the *Metalogicon* are canvassed by Keats-Rohan, "John of Salisbury and Education in Twelfth-Century Paris," 34, 35 notes 39, 42. Also see John of Salisbury, *Entheticus Maior and Minor*, ed. Jan van Laarhoven (hereafter *Entheticus*), 3 vols. (Leiden: Brill, 1987), 1:108 and John of Salisbury, *Historia Pontificalis*, ed. Marjorie Chibnall (Oxford: Oxford University Press, 1986), 16.

[24] *Metalogicon*, 20. In translating the *Metalogicon*, I have occasionally consulted D. D. McGarry's translation (Berkeley: University of California Press, 1955).

[25] *Metalogicon*, 81.

[26] Thus, David Luscombe in *The School of Peter Abelard* (Cambridge: Cambridge University Press, 1969) treats John as a reliable source for biographical details but not as a true intellectual heir to Abelard's ideas.

[27] *Metalogicon*, 116.

By contrast, John was less impressed by the masters to whom he turned following Abelard's departure from Mont-Sainte-Geneviève, namely, Alberic and Robert of Melun, with whom he studied in 1137 and 1138. The "Alberic" to whom John refers is presumably Alberic of Rheims, who had brought Abelard to trial in 1121, since John says of him that he "was in fact a most bitter foe of the nominalist sect."[28] John's dissatisfaction with Alberic stemmed from the teacher's tendency to discover problems and obscurities in even the most straightforward of teachings. By contrast, John complains of Robert of Melun (an Englishman who would be raised to bishop of Hereford during the Becket dispute and would become a defender of Henry II's cause) that his responses to difficult questions were answered quickly and with a minimum of verbiage (implying a superficiality of doctrine). John's appraisal of these two teachers is balanced, however, by the assertion that they were keen and diligent, and that the combination of their qualities into a single person would have produced the best disputant of the age. Each would have risen to true greatness, John concludes, had they learned more from their forebears and reveled less in the novelty of their own teachings.

John admits that by 1138 he had become convinced that his education in dialectic was complete and that he had learned all he needed to know. This arrogance was short-lived, however, as he quickly discovered that his knowledge was entirely rote. Returning to his senses, he says, he transferred to the study of grammar under the instruction of William of Conches, with whom he remained for three years. It seems that during the same period John also took lessons with Hardewin the German on the *quadrivium* and Thierry of Chartres on rhetoric.[29] Thus, by 1141, John had covered the subject-matter of the seven liberal arts, comprising the *trivium* and *quadrivium*.

Upon completion of this course of study, John determined to review and extend his basic grounding in the liberal arts—in effect, to pursue a post-graduate education—and undertook lessons with Richard l'Evêque, who enjoyed an apparently well-deserved reputation as a polymath.[30] At the same time, John felt himself prepared to move on to the "higher" subject of theology. He sought out Gilbert of Poitiers, from whom he received instruction in "logical and divine matters."[31] Although Gilbert, like Abelard, was soon to leave Paris and teaching (in his case, to become bishop of Poitiers in 1142), it is clear from John's remarks in the *Metalogicon* and *Historia Pontificalis* that he regarded this teacher to have made a particular impact upon him. In the former work, John quotes with approval Gilbert's condemnation of the superficial pursuit of philosophical

---

[28] *Metalogicon*, 71.

[29] *Metalogicon*, 72. Keats-Rohan's suggestion in "The Chronology of John of Salisbury's Studies in France," 199 that these lessons may have taken place before he enrolled with William does not seem probable, otherwise John would have already possessed a sufficiently broad training to recognize the conceit of believing that dialectic alone afforded him an adequate education.

[30] *Metalogicon*, 71–72.

[31] *Metalogicon*, 72.

and theological studies, which leads to students who are useless and unskilled.[32] He also cites Gilbert (along with Abelard) as an example of those thinkers of his own time who have been shunned by their contemporaries in spite of the originality and significance of their ideas.[33] Perhaps most importantly, the *Metalogicon* shows a direct debt in its positions to Gilbert's metaphysical and epistemological doctrines, to the extent that one recent scholar characterizes the project behind John's treatise as shaped by his teacher's philosophical program.[34]

The impression of an intellectual lineage is reinforced by the *Historia Pontificalis*, a large part of which narrates the heresy trial of Gilbert held at the Council of Rheims in 1148 and prosecuted by Bernard of Clairvaux and his devotees. At stake was the doctrine of the Trinity and related issues stemming from the doctrine of God that Gilbert had discussed in his commentary on Boethius's *De Trinitate*. John had witnessed the events about which he writes at first hand, and while he never speaks ill of Bernard (whose holy reputation led to his canonization in 1174), his sympathies with Gilbert are clear. The latter is described in one chapter as "the most learned man of our times," and elsewhere as "more subtle and profound than the rest."[35] John produces repeated encomia of Gilbert as a man of vast learning and an implacable opponent of heresy, claiming evidence from "intimate knowledge" and familiarity with lectures.[36] Moreover, John impugns the motives of some of the most vociferous detractors of Gilbert (including, ironically, his former teacher Robert of Melun) by questioning whether they might not have been motivated by professional jealousy or a desire to impress the powerful Bernard of Clairvaux.[37] To perhaps a greater extent than in the case of Abelard, John feels himself to stand within Gilbert's camp and to advocate his cause.

The departure of Gilbert to his new bishopric forced John to seek other teachers with whom to pursue his studies. He continued his theological lessons with his compatriot Robert Pullen until his elevation to the cardinalate in 1144;[38] thereafter, Simon of Poissy (also known as Simon of Paris) instructed him in theology.[39] Sometime during the same period, John also advanced his study of rhetoric with Peter Helias.[40]

---

[32] *Metalogicon*, 20.

[33] *Metalogicon*, 102.

[34] Clare Monagle, "Bookish Heresy: The Trial of Gilbert of Poitiers and Its Narratives" (M.A. Thesis, Department of History, Monash University, 1999), 99–127. Certainly, echoes of Gilbert's teaching on universals may be detected throughout the *Metalogicon*; and his teachings are also visible throughout Book 2 of the *Policraticus* in which John criticizes various forms of occultist practice popular in his day.

[35] *Historia Pontificalis*, 15, 28.

[36] *Historia Pontificalis*, 17–18, 28–29.

[37] *Historia Pontificalis*, 16.

[38] John may have known Pullen at Exeter, where he seems to have taught theology before moving to Oxford in 1133. See Orme, *Education in the West of England*, 23, 52.

[39] Smalley, *The Becket Conflict and the Schools*, 88–89.

[40] *Metalogicon*, 72.

A further intellectual force in John's life at Paris was another fellow Eng-lishman, Adam du Petit Pont, so named because of the bridge over the Seine near which he taught. John seems to have encountered Adam not as one of his teachers but as his colleague. The *Metalogicon* describes how its author, pov-erty-stricken and unable to rely upon family and friends for support, began to teach the sons of the nobility in order to meet the expenses of his own education. Although not explicit about when he started to give lessons himself, it was per-haps after 1141, but more probably after 1138, that he began to run short of funds.[41] John came to know Adam in the context of his self-admitted ignorance as a lecturer. Unable to answer all of the questions posed by his students, he had recourse to Adam, who shared his own knowledge with John and expounded, in particular, his understanding of Aristotle. Apparently the two became close, be-cause John was able to draw on Adam for information that was otherwise kept closely guarded and shared only with his disciples, a status that John disavows. John's attitude toward the substance of Adam's doctrine may best be described as ambivalent. On the one hand, he groups Adam with Gilbert and Abelard in one passage of the *Metalogicon*, but on the other hand, he chastises Adam for his obscurantism and needlessly arcane exposition of Aristotle.[42] The truth is likely as John says in Book 3 of the *Metalogicon*: they became friends, ex-changed books, and talked often, as academic colleagues are wont to do, but they also disagreed profoundly on many important issues (another enduring fea-ture of intellectual collegiality).[43]

John may not have been pleased, moreover, that Adam was ineffective at reining in the precociousness of William of Soissons, who is the only student mentioned by name in the *Metalogicon*. John claims that he taught introductory logic to William, then sent him on to Adam for advanced studies. John fears that it was under his friend Adam that William learned the bad intellectual habits that would eventually lead him to assert his unprecedented formulation of a new foundation for logical inquiry that demolished traditional reasoning and "the opinions of the ancients."[44] William is likely to be the "resident of the Petit Pont," mentioned in the *Entheticus Maior*, who rejects the writings of the an-cients in favor of the latest of his own inventions and discoveries.[45] Although the identity of John's other students has been a subject of speculation (Peter of

---

[41] *Metalogicon*, 72. On this point, see Keats-Rohan, "The Chronology of John of Salisbury's Studies in France," 199, who holds that John began teaching after 1138, i.e., while still studying with William of Conches. There is no reason to suppose, however, that "et quia" in the text necessarily means that John has resumed the narrative with Wil-liam, rather than Richard l'Evêque; indeed, the textual flow might imply the latter, since William of Conches has not been mentioned for a long spell nor is he ever directly re-ferred to again in the chapter.

[42] *Metalogicon*, 102, 142.

[43] *Metalogicon*, 114.

[44] *Metalogicon*, 72.

[45] *Entheticus Maior and Minor*, 1:108.

Celle, who became John's correspondent and confidant,[46] and Peter of Blois are two names that are occasionally floated), the fact that the only pupil whom he admits to be his own turned out so badly may explain his reluctance to continue teaching except as an expediency to meet his own costs.

Accompanying questions about the chronology of John's studies and his own instructional activities is the matter of his literary production during this period. Customarily, all of John's extant writings, with the exception of a few late letters, have been dated to a twenty-year span commencing in the mid-1150s. Recently, however, the hypothesis has been proposed that the first two sections of John's 1852-line philosophical and satirical poem, the *Entheticus de Dogmate Philosophorum* (or *Entheticus Maior*, denoting a distinction with the *Entheticus Minor*, a shorter version that prefaces the *Policraticus*), were composed in France while John was still a student.[47] Such verse was a common school exercise assigned by masters of grammar.[48] A temporal disjuncture in the composition of the poem would help to make sense of the clear disparity of tone and style between Parts I and II, which contain a stinging rebuke of the educational practices of some Paris teachers and a reconstruction of the doctrines of the ancient philosophers, and the third and fourth parts, which address the moral dangers of the court and public life.[49] As will be discussed in a subsequent section of this chapter, it seems likely that Parts III and IV (and also the short prologue) of the *Entheticus Maior* can be dated on the basis of internal and external evidence to a period between December 1154 and the summer of 1156 (and maybe no later than 1155).

When might John have composed Parts I and II? There is some internal evidence that may guide us. In Part I, John refers by name to Abelard, Robert of Melun, Alberic, William of Conches, and Adam du Petit Pont, as well as to the "resident of the Petit Pont" whom I have suggested may be William of Soissons.[50] None of John's known teachers after 1141 are mentioned. Thus John could not have begun to write the *Entheticus Maior* before 1141. The absence of

---

[46] See Ronald E. Pepin, "*Amicitia Jocosa*: Peter of Celle and John of Salisbury," *Florilegium* 5 (1983): 140–56; and John McLoughlin, "Amicitia in Practice: John of Salisbury and his Circle," in *England in the Twelfth Century*, ed. D. Williams (London: Boydell & Brewer, 1990), 165–80. Suspicion about a student-pupil relation between them has rightly been expressed by Lynn K. Barber, "Ecclesiology and the Twelfth-Century Church in the Letters of Peter of Celle" (M.A. Thesis, Department of History, University of North Carolina at Chapel Hill, 1978), 7–11.

[47] *Entheticus Maior and Minor*, 1:51.

[48] Stephen C. Ferruolo, *The Origins of the University: The Schools of Paris and Their Critics, 1100–1215* (Stanford: Stanford University Press, 1985), 93–130.

[49] Rodney Thomson, "What is the *Entheticus*?," in *WJS*, 294–95. Although the division into "Parts" is the work of later editors, this designation does reflect clear changes in the substance and presentation of the text. As a satirical commentary on the deteriorating conditions of education, Part I in particular falls within a well-established literary genre during the twelfth century, as many critics of contemporary instruction chose poetry to express their dismay, as Ferruolo points out.

[50] *Entheticus*, 1:108–9, 118–19.

references to later teachers might be taken as a sign that he composed at least Part I at the end of his three years of study with William of Conches, with whom he studied grammar, or perhaps soon thereafter while he was reviewing that subject under Richard l'Evêque. Certainly, the fact that he does not mention Gilbert of Poitiers, whose name is bracketed with Abelard in later works, seems significant. At minimum, one might imagine that John would have commented on Gilbert or his doctrines if he had written Parts I and II after 1147, when his former teacher had come under attack by Bernard of Clairvaux and his supporters. I propose, then, that regardless of whether they were written at the same time, or at different times, Part I and probably Part II have a *terminus a quo* of 1141 and a *terminus ad quem* of 1147, although John may have continued to revise the text into the 1150s.

In the Service of Canterbury (1148–1156)

In the prologue to the *Policraticus*, which seems to have been written in 1159 (during the siege of Toulouse), John laments that "almost twelve years" have been wasted on the frivolities of court.[51] Recalling John's statement in the *Metalogicon* that he spent twelve years beginning in 1136 pursuing his studies, it seems that his life took a dramatic turn from education to administration sometime in 1147. The dozen years thereafter mark the peak of John's creative activities as an author, even as he was also establishing himself as an ecclesiastical servant of prodigious talent and energy.

There has been considerable dispute among scholars about the sequence of events that led John away from the schools and into a courtly career.[52] The evidence suggests that in late 1147 he left Paris to reside with, and possibly work in a temporary position as clerk to, Abbot Peter of Celle, whom he probably knew in Paris, as noted before. A letter from the later 1150s from John to Peter expresses gratitude to the latter for supplying food and "kindness of old" at a time when the author was poor and without the support of parents.[53] Occasional references to John in Peter's letters as "our cleric," and John's mention of his presence in the company of Peter at Provins, a dependent house of Celle, hint that short-term administrative employment probably occupied him in 1147–1148.[54]

Why did John leave Paris? The most obvious reason was poverty, as John himself says in the letter to Peter. He may not have been able to earn sufficient keep as a teacher, hardly surprising given his rigorous attitude toward education

---

[51] Webb, 1:23.

[52] Avrom Saltman, *Theobald Archbishop of Canterbury* (London: Athlone Press, 1955), 169–75 provides a comprehensive survey of the issues and a definitive solution that shall be adopted here.

[53] John of Salisbury, *The Letters of John of Salisbury*, v. 1, ed. W. J. Millor, H. E. Butler, and C. N. L. Brooke (hereafter *Letters*, 1) (London: Thomas Nelson and Son, 1955), 55 (Letter 33).

[54] *Letters*, 1:xvii, 184 (Letter 112).

that was apparently not in keeping with the "market" for more superficial and utilitarian learning that prevailed in his day. Simply stated, John may not have been a very popular teacher because he demanded too much from his students.[55] At the same time, the educational environment in France was itself coming under attack. The successful suppression of Abelard seems to have emboldened powerful critics of the schools to indulge in inquisitional tactics. John's favorite master, Gilbert of Poitiers, had been charged with promulgating ideas inconsistent with orthodox belief, and the matter was initially examined before Pope Eugenius III at a council held in Paris at Easter 1147.[56] Was the prosecution of these charges—the culmination of which occurred at the Council of Rheims the following year—the final straw in John's growing trepidation about the decline of serious and thoughtful education at Paris? If so, John may have come to feel that an early exit from the schools was the better part of valor.

John in any case had the opportunity to view the consequences of Gilbert's prosecution in March and April of 1148 at Rheims. It was probably as Peter of Celle's agent that John attended the Council, perhaps with the aim of seeking employment in the service of one of the many dignitaries represented there. Whether Peter accompanied John to Rheims is uncertain, but unlikely, given that he wrote an account of the events many years after the fact (in the *Historia Pontificalis*) at the abbot's request. The care with which John observed the Council is indeed revealed by the *Historia Pontificalis*, which contains not only colorful accounts of the persons but also precise narration of arguments contributing to the condemnation of Gilbert.[57] If John held out any hope for an eventual return to study and education in the schools, whether at Paris or elsewhere, his witnessing of the trial of Gilbert surely confirmed his worst fears about the future of scholarly life.[58]

At the same time, John apparently succeeded in making an entrée into the world of ecclesiastical administration. Soon after the Council of Rheims ended, John returned to his native land, armed with a letter of recommendation from no less a personage than Bernard of Clairvaux addressed to Theobald, archbishop of Canterbury. Scholars have generally assumed that it was this letter from Bernard, whose eminence in Christendom by 1148 was so great that it would have been hard even for an archbishop to resist his request, that secured John his position at the court of Canterbury.[59]

Yet the incident is perhaps not so clear-cut as the conventional version would indicate. Bernard's recommendation of John was not sent to someone

---

[55] See the observations of Keats-Rohan, "John of Salisbury and Education in Twelfth-Century Paris," 25–27.

[56] *Historia Pontificalis*, 15–16.

[57] See Monagle, "Bookish Heresy," 78–85.

[58] Only once would John suggest a possible return to the schools of Paris—but this time, apparently, as an agent of Archbishop Thomas Becket, a plan that in any case never materialized; see *Letters*, 2:12–13 (Letter 136).

[59] *Letters*, 1:xv; Egbert Türk, *Nugae Curialium: Le règne d'Henri II Plantagenêt et l'éthique politique* (Geneva: Librairie Droz, 1977), 84–85; *Entheticus*, 5.

who was a close friend; he apparently met Theobald but once, at the Council of Rheims, and the letter was the only one he ever sent to Theobald. Moreover, its contents hardly constitute a ringing endorsement of John based on extensive personal knowledge.[60] It describes John as "the friend of my friends," having "a good reputation among good men," which Bernard claims to have learned about from his own intimates, "my sons whose words I believe as my own eyes," "reliable witnesses about his life and habits." In other words, Bernard's familiarity with John was almost entirely second-hand and indirect. As in so many other instances, Bernard relied upon his circle and coterie to act as his eyes and ears. Nor can John have been entirely enamored of Bernard, having just witnessed the conduct of the latter at the trial of his own master, Gilbert. There is a fine irony in the intellectual politics surrounding Bernard's letter of recommendation.

In light of the lack of intimacy between Bernard and John, one may well wonder how their contact had been facilitated. Here one might detect the hand of Peter of Celle, to whom John wrote in a letter: "It was thanks to you that I returned to the land of my birth; it was thanks to you that I have made acquaintance with the great, and have won the favor and the friendship of many."[61] The rest of the passage stresses John's extreme gratitude for Peter's efforts on his behalf, whereas John never in his writings acknowledges any debt to Bernard. It is not an implausible supposition that Peter, who had already become a figure of some influence in ecclesiastical politics by 1148 and who was in communication with Bernard, engineered John's introduction to him at the Council of Rheims toward the end of securing support for his friend's employment.[62]

In any event, Bernard's supplication of Theobald had the desired effect of providing for John "that he may have the means to live decently and honorably, and I beg you to do this without delay for he has nowhere to turn."[63] Theobald found in John a vigorous and dedicated champion of the cause of Canterbury, a see whose fortunes had waned earlier in the twelfth century.[64] Theobald had been an obscure monk of Bec (like his predecessors Anselm and Lanfranc) who had been consecrated archbishop of Canterbury in early 1139. Although technically primate of England, he had initially been forced to take a back seat to Henry of Blois, bishop of Winchester and brother of King Stephen. Until the death of Pope Innocent II in 1143, Henry held the office of papal legate in England, a position that severely constrained Theobald's ability to exercise the

---

[60] Bernard of Clairvaux, *The Letters of St. Bernard*, trans. Bruno S. James (Chicago: Henry Regnery, 1953), 459.

[61] *Letters,* 1:55 (Letter 33).

[62] Christopher Brooke, by contrast, thinks that "Bernard's favorite Parisian professor, the English Robert Pullen" had arranged the introduction; see "John of Salisbury and His World," in *WJS,* 8. But Pullen had not been teaching in Paris for several years at this point, and there is no evidence of their contact beyond 1144. Moreover, Brooke himself points out Peter of Celle's prestige and connection to Bernard in *Letters* 1:li.

[63] Bernard of Clairvaux, *Letters,* 459.

[64] The best source, and the one on which I shall rely heavily in what follows, remains Saltman, *Theobald.*

powers of his archepiscopacy. Thereafter, Theobald began to take a more active role in English affairs. He attempted repeatedly to mediate the raging civil war between Stephen and the supporters of Countess Matilda of Anjou, the former Empress, who was the daughter of Henry I and the original heir apparent to the throne of England. He also sought to unite the English bishops, who were split over the issue of royal succession, and to protect the collective liberties of the English church against repeated efforts to carve it up into multiple metropolitanates. Far from being the seat-warmer that many clerics had expected, Theobald proved to be among the most active and effective incumbents of Canterbury during the High Middle Ages.

Canterbury enjoyed a long reputation as a center of intellectual and political ferment, and Theobald's curia was hardly an exception.[65] Theobald seems to have been an especially acute spotter of administrative talent; many members of his circle went on to prominent positions as bishops both in England and on the continent. Thomas Becket may have been the most famous figure associated with Canterbury in Theobald's time, but he was joined by a large number of colleagues, at least some of whom would eventually oppose him after he became arch-bishop. Moreover, the court at Canterbury was extraordinarily cosmopolitan and many of its denizens were intellectually gifted. Training in the schools of France and Italy was a commonplace among members of Theobald's curia. Thus, amongst his Canterbury colleagues, John of Salisbury was by no means unusual in the extent of his travel and education. In turn, it was this brilliant circle that formed the primary audience for his output of writings during the 1150s. In his conduct at Canterbury, one might agree with Klaus Guth, John transformed his school lessons into a *Lebensform*, medieval humanism as a way of life.[66] By means of administrative service within such a literate and refined community, he was able to move seamlessly from theory to practice.

John's responsibilities at Canterbury were varied. At times, he was a diplomat, a secretary, a legal expert, and a trusted advisor—a sort of jack of all trades. Other than a charter that he witnessed sometime after he joined Theobald's curia in 1148,[67] we have no evidence of his activities for the first year or so in England. One assumes that John was learning the array of duties and tasks that occupied the servants of the archbishop. Perhaps he was also becoming familiar in an informal way with the basic principles of civil and canon law, since there is no evidence that he engaged in legal studies at Paris or elsewhere, yet some of his later letters (written under Theobald's signature) show a passing knowledge of the Corpus Juris Civilis and of Gratian's *Decretum*. John himself attests in the *Policraticus* to knowing the Italian canonist and civilian Vacarius, who resided in Theobald's household and also seems to have taught law in England.[68]

---

[65] See Guth, *Johannes von Salisbury*, 111–66.

[66] Klaus Guth, "Hochmittelalterlicher Humanismus als Lebensform: ein Beitrag zum Standesethos des westeuropäischen Weltklerus nach Johannes von Salisbury," in *WJS*, 63–76.

[67] Saltman, *Theobald*, 170.

[68] Webb 2:399; see *Letters*, 1:xxiii; Saltman, *Theobald*, 175; Max Kerner,

John's earliest established duties for Theobald were diplomatic. In the middle of 1149, he traveled to the curia of Pope Eugenius III, who was probably resident in Rome. It has been speculated that his goal was the promotion of Theobald's efforts to have himself designated the papal legate in England. Such an appointment, which was granted in 1150, solidified Theobald's authority over his fellow ecclesiastical lords as well as improving his ability to negotiate and impose a lasting peace in the civil war.[69] For the next four or more years, John journeyed regularly across the English Channel to the courts of successive popes, wherever they were domiciled, in the service of Canterbury's interests. By one count, he was on the continent for extended periods a total of five times by 1154, including his first visit in 1149.[70] Such lengthy stays away from Canterbury mean that John would have had little direct involvement in the settlement between King Stephen and his enemies that Theobald brokered and that was concluded in 1153.

John's diplomatic activities were supplemented, although never entirely replaced, by work as secretary to Theobald, authoring correspondence in matters pertaining to ecclesiastical business, an assignment that would soon keep him at Canterbury for longer periods of time. The earliest letters written by John for Theobald seem to date to 1153/1154, and their flow increases rapidly by 1156. Perhaps not coincidentally, it is also at this time that King Stephen died and the crown passed to his negotiated heir, Henry, the son of Empress Matilda and Geoffrey of Anjou. Archdeacon Thomas Becket, whom Theobald held in high esteem as an important member of his curia, almost immediately received appointment as Henry's chancellor, an act that Saltman plausibly regards as a favor on the part of the new king to the archbishop.[71] The concurrence of these events affords prima facie reason to suppose that many of the administrative tasks with which Becket had busied himself at Canterbury were turned over to John, although he acquired no office (such as archdeacon, which Becket retained) or title commensurate with his responsibilities.

It remains a widely held view that John and Becket were close friends throughout their careers. This supposition is seen to be confirmed by later events, such as John's support in the conflict with Henry II and his efforts to canonize Thomas, not to mention the dedication of both the *Policraticus* and the *Metalogicon* to Becket. Yet the evidence for this intimacy at an early date is sparse. There is no documentation that Becket knew John from school days in

---

"Römisches und kirchliches Recht im *Policraticus*," in *WJS*, 376–78; idem, "Johannes von Salisbury und das gelehrte Recht," in *Proceedings of the Ninth International Congress of Medieval Canon Law*, ed. Peter Landau and Joers Mueller, Monumenta Iuris Canonici Subsidia 10 (Vatican City: Biblioteca Apostolica Vaticana, 1997), 503–21; and R. W. Southern, *Scholastic Humanism and the Unification of Europe*, v. 2 (Oxford: Blackwell, 2001), 155–66.

[69] Saltman, *Theobald*, 30–32. Also see Southern, *Scholastic Humanism and the Unification of Europe*, 2:167–77.

[70] *Letters*, 1:253–56.

[71] Saltman, *Theobald*, 168.

Paris, prior to the arrival of the latter at Canterbury.[72] When John came to Canterbury, Becket had already been in Theobald's service for some time and was further along the *cursus honorum*. In Frank Barlow's estimation, the personalities of John and Thomas were so different that Becket would have found his colleague "culturally, if not intellectually, intimidating."[73] Becket's background and temperament were those of a practical man and one who was early on reputed for his worldliness, someone who was perhaps not inclined to take part in the life of the mind that John revered as the hallmark of the Canterbury circle.[74] Thomas may have been very much an outsider in the refined corridors of Canterbury.

It is not implausible to suppose, then, that the two men's relationship during the late 1140s and 1150s was largely a professional one. In the first period of John's service to Theobald, he was physically absent from Canterbury for extended periods of time even as Thomas was building his career under the archbishop. After 1155, when John became more settled in England, Becket's work as chancellor kept him almost constantly in the king's company, which placed him overseas from January 1156 to April 1157 and again after August 1158.[75] If John viewed Thomas as an intimate distanced from him by circumstance, one might expect a significant volume of correspondence between them. Unlike exchanges with friends such as Peter of Celle and even Pope Adrian IV (the Englishman Nicholas Brakespear)—often long meditations incorporating witty and sophisticated repartee and classical allusions—John's personal letters to Thomas (of which only two prior to 1161 are recorded in John's collection) are businesslike and straightforward. The first letter entreats Becket to intervene for John in restoring the good will of Henry II; the other contains a desperate plea for Thomas to return from the continent to Canterbury to visit the mortally ill Theobald.[76] The circumstances of the former letter are particularly troubling. Having fallen afoul of Henry in late 1156 for reasons that remain somewhat obscure, John composed a letter that beseeches Becket's assistance in resolving the dispute. But John so lacked confidence in his influence that he sent the letter not directly to Thomas, but instead to Becket's secretary, Ernulf, along with a separate cover note begging him to ensure the chancellor's attention and intercession.[77]

John's admiration for, yet personal distance from, Becket arguably echoes in the third and fourth parts (and also the prologue) of the *Entheticus Maior*, sections that seem most likely to have been completed between the appointment of Thomas as royal chancellor and the middle of 1156. It was during this period that the expectations of John and others of his circle would have been at their highest for Becket's adherence to the cause of Theobald as he sought to uphold and strengthen the authority of Canterbury. Parts III and IV of the *Entheticus*

---

[72] Frank Barlow, *Thomas Becket* (London: Weidenfeld and Nicolson, 1986), 20.

[73] Barlow, *Thomas Becket*, 32.

[74] *Letters*, 2:516–17 (Letter 256).

[75] This has been stressed by van Laarhoven in *Entheticus*, 1:49.

[76] *Letters*, 1:45–46 (Letter 28), 221–23 (Letter 128). John also authored two letters for Theobald to Becket (Letters 22 and 129).

[77] *Letters*, 1:44 (Letter 27).

Maior are on the model of a poetic courtly *speculum*: the third part describes the unsavory characters one encounters in public life, while the fourth part admonishes its reader about how the good courtier should behave. That Becket was the intended recipient of the treatise can be established independently of the addendum to the *explicit* of the exemplar manuscript British Library, Royal 13 D. IV that reads: "written for Thomas the chancellor, later archbishop of Canterbury" (an emendation made in another hand, probably between 1162 and 1170).[78] Reference is made to Becket in undisguised or thinly veiled terms throughout the third and fourth sections; in Part III, in particular, the "chancellor" is identified as the commissioner and "patron" of the poem.[79] John evinces optimism that Thomas can negotiate the snares of Henry's court and return in good moral condition to take his rightful place in Canterbury.

It is precisely such an optimistic outlook that may point to the correct dating of the *Entheticus Maior* in its more or less final form. Scholars generally conclude that Becket's rapid appointment as chancellor was engineered by Theobald as a means to control the young king and to ensure renewed royal respect for the liberties of the church and the archepiscopacy.[80] Becket was, in short, planted as an agent of Canterbury's cause.[81] In this role, however, he soon became a noteworthy disappointment, as scholarship usually attests.[82] Becket's loyalties quickly changed along with his personality, and far from being the leading voice favoring ecclesiastical liberty in Henry's administration, he became one of the most notorious abusers of church privileges, often to his own profit.[83] John's poem reflects none of these developments, suggesting that the courtly sections were authored early in Becket's chancellorship, before his transformation was fully apparent. Certainly, this points to a date prior to mid-1156, by which time Theobald had openly opposed and reproached Becket concerning the so-called "second aid" controversy.[84]

---

[78] Thomson, "What is the *Entheticus*?," 290.

[79] *Entheticus*, 1:188–89, 200–1, 202–5.

[80] John himself hints at this in his *Vita Sancti Thomae*, ed. G. A. Giles (London: Whittaker and Company, 1845), 1:321. The customary view (stemming from the work of Z. N. Brooke) that Henry followed a program of threatening ecclesiastical liberties has been challenged by W. L. Warren, *Henry II* (Berkeley: University of California Press, 1973), 427–46. For a rebuke to this position, see Natalie M. Fryde, "The Roots of Magna Carta: Opposition to the Plantagenets," in *Political Thought and the Realities of Power in the Middle Ages*, ed. Joseph Canning and Otto Gerhard Oexle (Göttingen: Vandenhoeck and Ruprecht, 1998), 53–65.

[81] Saltman, *Theobald*, 168; Christopher Brooke, *Medieval Church and Society* (London: Sidgwick and Jackson, 1971), 131.

[82] David Knowles, *Thomas Becket* (London: Adam and Charles Black, 1970), 27–29; Brooke, *Medieval Church and Society*, 124–25; Barlow, *Thomas Becket*, 44–45.

[83] See Cary J. Nederman and Arlene Feldwick, "To the Court and Back Again: The Origins and Dating of the *Entheticus de Dogmate Philosophorum* of John of Salisbury," *Journal of Medieval and Renaissance Studies* 21 (1991): 129–45, here 133–34.

[84] *Letters*, 1:35–36 (Letter 22).

Nor is the role played by Becket in the *Entheticus Maior* the only evidence for dating of Parts III and IV to the period between late 1154 and the middle of 1156. To posit a later composition of those sections would clash with several elements of thematic analysis. Beginning in late 1156, we know that John had commenced writing the *Policraticus*, starting with the meditations on philosophy and fortune that constitute most of Books 7 and 8 of the final version. If John was working on the third and fourth sections of the *Entheticus Maior* at about the same time, then its tone and themes are at odds with the prose work. The reflections of the *Entheticus Maior* are far less introspective than the seventh and eighth books of the *Policraticus*: the former is a work of advice to another, whereas the latter is a treatise of self-consolation in the manner of Boethius. The key themes of the initially composed chapters of the *Policraticus* are the nature of fortune and its overcoming. The *Entheticus Maior* discusses fortune only once and in a rather abstract fashion, for fourteen lines in Part I, which, as we have seen, is likely to have been composed in the 1140s. It seems plausible to explain the disparity between the texts by John's fall from favor with Henry II, an event that occurred in late 1156. The poem's concerns about earthly corruption serve to illuminate its author's moral lessons, not to assuage his private agony.

Perhaps the greatest difficulty with dating Parts III and IV of the *Entheticus Maior* to any time after the middle of 1156 is the author's evident fascination with the reign of King Stephen and its relative lack of comment on Henry's court. In John's one unambiguous reference to the Angevin ruler, he warns against the dangers presented by "the new court (*nova curia*) under a boy king (*rege sub puero*)."[85] The use of the term *puer* in and of itself does not constitute evidence of the age of Henry (twenty-one years when he acceded) or the date of the text, as van Laarhoven has already demonstrated.[86] But the coupling of *puer* with *nova curia* (upon which van Laarhoven makes no remark) suggests more directly that Henry is in the earliest stages of his reign, when his court has only recently been formed.

By contrast, John has far more to say about the rule of King Stephen, whose identity scholars have detected in the (Maccabean) pseudonym "Hircanus."[87] To Hircanus John devotes more than fifty lines of poetic condemnation, while his courtiers are reviled to an even greater extent.[88] Despite Ronald Pepin's suggestion that "Hircanus" is a pun on "Henricus,"[89] John's character is clearly a king whose reign has ended; the past tense is employed throughout the passage in question. Moreover, the description of Hircanus's negligence accords closely

---

[85] *Entheticus*, 1:200.

[86] *Entheticus*, 2:389.

[87] *Entheticus*, 2:377–78; Phyllis Barzillay, "The *Entheticus de Dogmate Philosophorum* of John of Salisbury," *Medievalia et Humanistica* 16 (1964): 20–21 and note 77; and Liebeschütz, *Mediaeval Humanism in the Life and Writings of John of Salisbury*, 21–22.

[88] *Entheticus*, 1:190–98.

[89] Ronald E. Pepin, "John of Salisbury's *Entheticus* and the Classical Tradition of Satire," *Florilegium* 3 (1981): 215–27, here 221.

with John's description in *Policraticus* 6.18 of the political chaos that occasioned Stephen's reign.[90] That Stephen, not Henry, should be the central target of John's wrath seems strange if the final version of the *Entheticus Maior* was stimulated by his banishment from court in late 1156. A date of composition that locates the texts in the initial eighteen months of Henry's rule more adequately explains the concentration upon Stephen. The evil customs and policies initiated under Stephen's reign constituted a far more tangible threat in the minds of the Canterbury circle to the well-being of the English church than any potential machinations on the part of the "boy king" whose accession had enjoyed the support of the archbishop and who was presumed to be under the guidance of Theobald's faithful minion, Becket. For John, the situation would have changed dramatically in later 1156; thereafter, Henry and his court could no longer be trusted to act in the interests of the church and its loyal servants. Only if we accept that Parts III and IV of the *Entheticus Maior* were composed after Christmastide 1154 but before the tumultuous events of late 1156 can those sections of the text be understood in a historically coherent manner.

Author and Administrator (1157–1161)

In late 1155, John again traversed the English Channel and made his way to Benevento in Apulia where the papal curia was in residence. His intimate, Nicholas Brakespear, had been elevated as Pope Adrian IV the previous year. John's assignment, as he himself says, was at least in part to help secure the terms under which Henry II might procure a papal grant of Ireland as a hereditary fee in preparation for an invasion.[91] Although it has customarily been presumed that these negotiations were at Henry's behest,[92] W. L. Warren has detected in the process the hand of Theobald, who had a very direct interest in reasserting English control over bishops in the Norse townships of Ireland, where the hegemony of Canterbury had lapsed since 1140.[93] If so, it may have been Theobald and his agents who sought to use Pope Adrian's authority to encourage Henry to pursue an agenda that most of all favored the rights of the archbishop. Certainly, this is implied in the tone of Adrian's bull *Laudabiliter*, which not merely permits but positively pronounces that Henry act against Ireland "for the increase of the Christian religion."[94]

---

[90] Cary J. Nederman, "The Changing Face of Tyranny: The Reign of King Stephen in John of Salisbury's Political Thought," *Nottingham Medieval Studies* 33 (1989): 1–20.

[91] *Metalogicon*, 183; that this may not have been John's only purpose at the papal court is clear from his remark in the *Policraticus* (Webb 2:67) that he consulted with the pope during this trip regarding "many matters," including their famous exchange about the debased condition of the church and the papal court.

[92] Giles Constable, "The Alleged Disgrace of John of Salisbury in 1159," *English Historical Review* 69 (1954): 67–76, here 67–69.

[93] Warren, *Henry II*, 195.

[94] Quoted in Warren, *Henry II*, 195–96, after which the conclusion is drawn that the document "reads more like an attempt to encourage a hesitant king."

Upon John's return to England in the spring of 1156, he once again takes up his function as a secretary to Theobald. We possess several letters from the summer and fall of that year written by John for the archbishop. Then, suddenly, John writes to his friends Adrian IV and Peter of Celle that he has fallen afoul of Henry. To the pope, John says simply—and almost in passing, between other news—that "the bishop of Lisieux" has aroused in the king "such a storm of indignation against myself, your servant, that it is not safe for me to remain in England and impossible, or at least very difficult, for me to leave it."[95] Arnulf of Lisieux was at this time an intimate of the king (although later he, too, would know Henry's wrath), and was one of the members of the royal mission who were at Benevento when the terms of the Irish settlement were addressed.[96] The prima facie evidence points to John's activities at Adrian's court, pushing the interests of Canterbury upon an all-too-willing pope, as the reason for the wrath of the king. Arnulf had accused John, in effect, of dictating royal foreign policy under the guise of religious fervor for the sake of improving Theobald's (and Rome's) strength and standing within the church.

This interpretation accords with the facts laid out by John in a longer narration of events recounted to Peter of Celle. John tells Peter that "after I returned from the church of Rome, Fortune piled on me such a load of bitter troubles that I think I have never before endured anything to call trouble." Reporting that King Henry "has grown hot against me in full force," he explains the reason: "I favored him more than was just and worked for his advancement with greater vigor than I should have."[97] One might understand this as a reference to John's efforts to magnify the power of the English crown by seeking a papal mandate for expansion into Ireland, however much the scheme also served the interests of Canterbury. In consequence of his conduct—the innocence of which he loudly proclaims—John announces the rather vague terms of his supposed crime. "I alone in all the realm am accused of diminishing the royal dignity," he asserts, in particular by defending the rights and liberties of the Roman and English churches, "as if I were the only person to instruct the lord archbishop of Canterbury and the other bishops what they ought to do."[98] John, in other words, believes that Arnulf has spread the word that John is the force behind ecclesiastical attempts to manipulate Henry and deprive him of royal authority. In a letter to Adrian dated to early 1157, John repeats the charge that "the bishop of Lisieux is a hammer of iniquity in order to break the church of God in pieces. He has heaped up the king's indignation against my poor self to such an extent that the king himself has denounced me to both the archbishop of Canterbury and to his chancellor for abasing the royal dignity; and for this reason he asserts that I should be excluded from among the number of his friends and faithful subjects."[99] Henry's attitude persists, John claims, in spite of the pope's efforts to

---

[95] *Letters*, 1:30 (Letter 18).
[96] Constable, "The Alleged Disgrace of John of Salisbury," 67.
[97] *Letters*, 1:31 (Letter 19).
[98] *Letters*, 1:32 (Letter 19).
[99] *Letters*, 1:48 (Letter 30).

assuage the king; indeed, in light of the Irish situation, a papal commendation might well have fanned, rather than dampened, the fire of royal anger.

John reports his quandary about how to proceed. In his initial letter to Peter of Celle, he expresses the fear that he is in danger of banishment and proposes to leave England before the beginning of the new year, to take up residence either in France or at the papal curia.[100] John also seeks in vain to attract support for his cause from Becket via his secretary Ernulf, an unlikely strategy not least because the archbishop of Canterbury was at just that moment feuding with the archdeacon over his attempt to exact a "second aid" from the churches directly subject to the archbishop. Becket would hardly have looked kindly on a request for assistance from someone so closely tied to Theobald. In April of 1157, John continues to fret about his best course of action. Another letter to Peter contains further musing about the whims of Fortune, repeats the charges maliciously made against him, and reports the discovery that the king will not admit John into his presence without first consulting the archbishop about his reliability.[101] John has restrained himself from going into exile on the advice of friends, including the pope. "To leave the island might suggest that I was a fugitive," John reflects; "to refuse to meet my calumniators might seem to argue a guilty conscience; not to await the sight of my ruler [Henry is overseas] might expose me to the laws of high treason."[102] There is a faint promise that the "storm" that has engulfed John's life will soon blow over (Henry's quick temper and quick forgiveness were famous even in his early years), but he awaits the result.[103] Only in John's next letter to Peter, four or five months later, does it seem that Henry has signaled his pardon, as he has passed through England on the way to his campaign against Wales.[104] There is no direct recounting of how John's restoration to Henry's good graces occurred, but no evidence is found in later correspondence that his relationship with the king was in permanent disrepair. Throughout this period of political uncertainty, which may have lasted for as long as eight months, John was effectively paralyzed in carrying out his work for Theobald. Banished from Henry's court, he could not transact the business of Canterbury with royal officials. Yet he was loath to travel overseas as the archbishop's agent for fear of incurring the king's further wrath. John was, to use his own words stated to Adrian IV, "twice an exile" insofar as he was an "exile in his home."[105]

John's direct encounter with the harm that courtly machinations might cause seems to have jolted him into a serious frame of mind. It was one thing to satirize the foibles and follies of courtiers, as he had done in the *Entheticus Maior*. To have one's career and reputation endangered by the whispers of some personal or political enemy, however, suggested the need for more serious consideration of his

---

[100] *Letters*, 1:32 (Letter 19).
[101] *Letters*, 1:49–50 (Letter 31).
[102] *Letters*, 1:50 (Letter 31).
[103] *Letters*, 1:51 (Letter 31).
[104] *Letters*, 1:52–53 (Letter 32).
[105] *Letters*, 1:34 (Letter 21).

circumstances. Accordingly, John began at the end of 1156 to compose a prose work that attempted to demonstrate the foundations of the good human life and to demystify the false images of happiness propounded by those of his contemporaries who unwittingly advocated the hedonistic doctrines of the Epicureans. This treatise, following the format of philosophical self-consolation modeled on Boethius's *Consolation of Philosophy*, came to form the basis of John's *Policraticus*. First an unfinished dissertation by Gerhard W. Bonhage (summarized in print by Georg Miczka), and then Max Kerner's analysis of the internal structure of the *Policraticus*, have convincingly identified Book 7, Prologue and Chapters 1–16 and 25 and Book 8, Prologue and Chapters 1–14, 24, and part of 25 as the work of late 1156 (perhaps up through the resolution of John's dispute with Henry in the spring or summer of 1157).[106] The language and concerns of these chapters clearly echo John's letters during the period of royal disfavor, developing in more complete fashion some of the philosophical themes that he had first begun to explore in the *Entheticus Maior*.

John laments the lack of opportunity that his administrative tasks have afforded him to write and adopt the mantle of the philosopher. But now that fortune has struck him down, he admits that perhaps his sorrows may be assuaged by putting pen to parchment.[107] John's remarks are addressed to someone who "exhorts him to write," whose identity has been assumed to be Becket, since it is the latter to whom the final version of the *Policraticus* is dedicated. Given the lack of communication between them in 1156 occasioned by Becket's absence from England, however, one wonders whether the exhortation does not have some closer (and more philosophically inclined) source than Thomas. This would make the initial treatise analogous to the *Metalogicon*, which was also sent to Becket but in which John asserts that "my companions wished it" for him to compose the work.[108] There is no reason to suppose, in other words, that Becket provided the original stimulus, even if he formed the final audience, for John's writing.

The perspective espoused in the sections of the *Policraticus* dated to the period of royal disfavor, while replete with scriptural references, concentrates upon the doctrines of the ancient philosophers. John declares his devotion to the viewpoint of the New Academy, with its commitment to a moderate, anti-dogmatic skepticism. He then surveys the doctrines of the major schools of classical philosophy as he knows them, and explores the ways in which a philosophical education is useful to the promotion of wisdom and virtue as well as how such instruction should proceed. John closes this part of his meditation on fortune with a defense of intellectual and moral liberty consistent with his Academic stance. A second part, containing the sections that would be integrated into Book 8 of the *Policraticus*, opens with a second prologue again adopting a

---

[106] Georg Miczka, *Das Bild der Kirche bei Johannes von Salisbury* (Bonn: Ludwig Röhrscheid Verlag, 1970), 7; Max Kerner, *Johannes von Salisbury und die Logische Struktur seines Policraticus* (Wiesbaden: Franz Steiner Verlag, 1977), 114–16.

[107] Webb 2:91–92.

[108] *Metalogicon*, 10.

personal form of address. No reason exists, however, to assume that Becket is the addressee. The latter part concerns "the camp of the Epicureans," in which John includes "those who are in all things slaves to their own wills."[109] Epicurean teaching is for him the root of all vice, personal as well as public; he advocates in its place a model of civility and decorum in one's consumption, sexual pursuits, and expenditures. Epicureanism proves to be self-defeating, because it never leads to happiness, whereas John's path assures human fulfillment. Thus, John consoles himself (and his readers) that his bitter treatment at the hands of fortune is of no importance to one who shuns Epicurean values. Indeed, a philosophically informed way of life, founded on wisdom and virtue, always soundly defeats the ill winds of misfortune.

From the leisure that the few months of royal disfavor conferred upon him, John was thrown back into the whirlwind of court politics. Theobald had grown physically incapacitated over the course of the 1150s, and relied ever more heavily upon his staff to stand in for him. Without Becket's assistance, John seems to have become the archbishop's closest aide. In the final chapter of the *Metalogicon*, written in late 1159, John explains his circumstances to Becket: "Theobald, the venerable archbishop of Canterbury, has fallen gravely ill, so much so that it is doubtful what can be hoped or what should be feared. He can no longer supervise business as in the past, and he has committed to me the province, and he has imposed the insupportable burden of supervising all ecclesiastical affairs."[110] The evidence of John's letters written on Theobald's behalf would seem to confirm this claim. Whereas prior to late 1156 John had dealt with only a handful of cases for Theobald, the flow of work from 1157 through to the archbishop's death in 1161 increases exponentially. Of the letters that can be dated with any certainty, most fall into the final two years of Theobald's archepiscopacy. It has been surmised that John made a final trip on Canterbury's behalf to Rome in 1158, explaining the relative dearth of letters assignable to that year and early 1159. In any case, by later in 1159, John had been left to cope with disputes internal to the English church as well as with the business stemming from Canterbury's relations with the king and papacy. Clearly, Theobald placed a great deal of trust in his secretary, as evidenced by his choice of John to draft his will as well as to serve (along with the archbishop's brother, his chancellor, and another member of the Canterbury circle) as one of its executors.[111]

Yet, in spite of John's administrative duties, he continued with his own writing as time permitted. Sometime after he drafted his little treatise on fortune and philosophy, he began to compose the full text of the *Policraticus*, a draft of which he sends to Peter of Celle in late summer or early autumn of 1159.[112] Scholars have tended to treat Books 1 through 6 as largely undifferentiated products of John's free time over a two-year period, perhaps with the finishing touches (the poetic prologue *Entheticus Minor*, as well as the Chapters 7–14 of

---

[109] Webb, 2:227.
[110] *Metalogicon*, 184.
[111] *Letters*, 1:245 (Letter 134).
[112] *Letters*, 1:182 (Letter 111).

Book 7 and 15–23 of Book 8) added as late as the summer of 1160.[113] Beyond this, the dating has remained vague. A somewhat more precise chronology consistent with the evidence as we know it may be possible, however. The work of Janet Martin has demonstrated beyond doubt that the lauded erudition of the *Policraticus* depended heavily upon John's access to the library facilities at Canterbury, in particular, *florilegia* and other volumes that were held by Christ Church and St. Augustine's Abbey.[114] The contents of the *Policraticus*, in other words, directly reflect the textual location of John's sources, a view reinforced by his emphasis in the prologue upon his heavy reliance upon the best authorities.[115] Assuming that John was in Italy during later 1158 and/or early 1159, it seems unlikely that he was able to make much progress on the text in that time. He further indicates in the prologue that the work was composed over a long period of time, and apologizes for its unevenness, which is "to be ascribed to matters of employment, that is, those affairs of court by which I am distracted to the extent that one is hardly allowed any time to write."[116] John also complains in his September or October letter to Peter of Celle that Brito, a monk at Canterbury, had held onto the manuscript for a long time and had it copied for his own purposes.[117] On the basis of this evidence, I would propose that John had completed the substance of the *Policraticus* Books 1–6 (and much of the unfinished parts of Books 7 and 8) in the year or more following his return to Henry's favor but before his overseas mission to Rome in 1158 and/or 1159. He does not seem to have been overwhelmed with administrative work during this time, and clearly had access to the Canterbury libraries. John lent the draft to Brito either before he left for the continent or perhaps immediately upon his return. Once he had wrested it back from the monk, he added the final flourishes of the prologue and closing chapter that contain references to recent events in Becket's life, then shipped the completed version off to Peter of Celle for his criticism and comments.

This sequence of the composition of the *Policraticus* must be correlated with what may be surmised about the composition of the *Metalogicon*, which is generally dated to the same period. The final chapter of the *Metalogicon* refers explicitly to the siege of Toulouse, the death of Adrian IV and ensuing papal schism, and the grave illness of Theobald, indicating its completion after the middle of September but not later than early or mid-October.[118] When John started it has been more difficult to establish. Scholars have generally treated it as a work contemporaneous with the *Policraticus*. Indeed, some have imagined that the two treatises were originally intended to be a single encyclopedic work—an expansion of the themes of the *Entheticus Maior*—which John later

---

[113] Miczka, *Das Bild der Kirche*, 7; Kerner, *Johannes von Salisbury und die Logische Struktur*, 116–19.

[114] This important discovery, revealed in a doctoral dissertation and several articles, is summarized in Janet Martin, "John of Salisbury as Classical Scholar," in *WJS*, 179–201.

[115] Keats-Rohan, 24–25.

[116] Keats-Rohan, 26.

[117] *Letters*, 1:182 (Letter 111).

[118] *Metalogicon*, 183–84.

divided into separate projects.[119] While John does indeed return to the major issues of the *Entheticus Maior* in his two later books, there is no external evidence for the claim that his original intent was to produce a single, more extensive prose version of his satirical poem. Indeed, given what we now know about the circumstances of the composition of the *Policraticus*, not to mention its thematic integrity and cohesion, such a hypothesis seems highly implausible.[120] Despite significant conceptual overlap between the *Metalogicon* and *Policraticus*,[121] we are not warranted in inferring a common origin.

When, then, was the *Metalogicon* composed? There are a few hints that may guide us. In his prologue, John explains that he wrote the work to refute an "opponent" who was constantly chastising him about the worthlessness of a liberal arts curriculum, especially an education in logic. In order to satisfy his friends, he says, he produced the *Metalogicon* by way of response. Unlike the *Policraticus*, however, John says that the *Metalogicon* was a work of the moment, composed under duress: "I had almost to throw the words together, since I had neither the leisure nor the energy to enter into a subtle examination of opinions nor to refine the words." He goes on to state what he will repeat in the final chapter, namely, that he is entirely consumed with his "regular occupation" of serving Theobald by taking over his ecclesiastical duties. Coping with such responsibilities and juggling court politics has left him no time for the sustained study that might have produced a more polished work. John thus begs not to be judged too harshly for the superficiality of his statements.[122]

John returns to some of these points in the preface to the third book of the *Metalogicon*, but important differences emerge. As in the initial prologue, he refers to being prodded by an adversary into making some defense of higher learning. He explains his own intellectual inadequacies by reference to his advanced age, the years separating him from his own education, and the distractions of traveling throughout Europe and England in the service of Canterbury. Nothing of the breathless intensity of the immediate circumstances at Canterbury is suggested here. Most significantly, John says that "nearly (*fere*) twenty years have elapsed" since he had ceased to study logic on account of the pressures of finance and the counsels of his friends.[123] Since his impoverishment may have commenced as early as 1138, this statement may have been written as early as 1156 or 1157. In general, the preface to Book 3 covers much of the same ground as the prologue. It must be kept in mind, as well, that the third book and the first six chapters of the fourth book of the *Metalogicon* are comprised of detailed commentaries on the major tracts of scholastic logic, primarily

---

[119] *Letters*, 1:xliv–xlv; Christopher Elrington, "John of Salisbury's 'Entheticus de Dogmate Philosophorum'" (M.A. Thesis, University of London, 1954), quoted by Kerner, *Johannes von Salisbury und die Logische Struktur*, 111.

[120] This is supported by the manuscript evidence as well; see Keats-Rohan, xi.

[121] An especially persuasive case for this is made by Michael Wilks, "John of Salisbury and the Tyranny of Nonsense," in *WJS*, 263–86.

[122] *Metalogicon*, 10.

[123] *Metalogicon*, 101–2.

Aristotle's *Organon*. John says in the preface to Book 3 that these chapters form summaries of his reading as a youth, the reminiscence of which brings him great pleasure.[124] The rest of Book 4 (except chapter 42) is a more general analysis of the nature of human intellectual properties, especially reason, that is derived from an eclectic set of sources. The final chapter of the book contains the dedication to Becket and news of recent events.

The changes in tone and substance—from the general and combative polemic of the first and second (and also some of the fourth) books to the more placid exposition of Book 3 and the initial chapters of Book 4—hint at different circumstances of composition. Given what we have concluded about John's proclivity for writing his works piecemeal, there is some plausibility in proposing that John began to draft parts of the *Metalogicon* at a time earlier than about 1159. Certainly, Book 3 and Book 4, chapters 1–6 could have been composed as school notes when he was still a student in Paris, although they probably reflect his attempt to reconstruct his education in the mid-1150s (almost two decades after he halted his study of logic) as opportunity and access to Aristotle's writings permitted.[125] Chapters 7–41 of Book 4 appear to draw more general conclusions from the commentaries on Aristotle necessary for responding to John's "opponent." The third and fourth books approach, then, a self-contained unit. In light of this reconstruction, it seems that John, who was in the midst of his heavy administrative duties on behalf of Theobald, hastily wrote the first and second books, and definitely chapter 42 of Book 4, only later. These date to the time after the archbishop had fallen ill but before the failure of the siege of Toulouse came to be known in England, that is, possibly while John was overseas in Rome but probably following his return in late 1158 or early 1159.

There is some further internal evidence to support this more specific dating of the *Metalogicon*. The text as we have it contains two explicit references to the *Policraticus*: one to John's critique of the "frivolities of courtiers," the other to his condemnation of occult arts.[126] Both of these references are in Book 1 of the *Metalogicon*. By contrast, the *Policraticus* contains no direct mention of the *Metalogicon* as a titled treatise. A cogent supposition—assuming that the direct citations in the text were not a later addition—is that the *Policraticus* was substantially completed before John turned his hand to at least the first book of the *Metalogicon*. If the former was done before the end of 1158, then the latter was probably not composed until at least late in that year. Further evidence about the viability of this hypothesis might be ascertained from additional investigation into the *Metalogicon*'s sources along the lines of Martin's research on the *Policraticus*.

There are additional compelling reasons, intellectual as well as biographical, to posit a more expansive chronology for the composition of John's major works. As John tells us, he was a busy administrator who became far more occupied as the 1150s passed. To view both the *Metalogicon* and the *Policraticus* as entirely or

---

[124] *Metalogicon*, 103.

[125] John still did not possess personal copies of the Aristotelian corpus in the mid-1160s; see *Letters*, 2:294–295 (Letter 201).

[126] *Metalogicon*, 19, 29.

largely the work of the same period strikes one as implausible. Rather, it seems to fit the facts better to conclude that the works were composed more slowly from at least the period of John's falling out with Henry's court, when he had several months of free time, up to late in 1159, when we know him to be burdened with Theobald's responsibilities. Thus, although always separate in composition, the two treatises evolved in an organic relationship with each other, the ideas of the one helping to bolster the doctrines of the other.

This supports Peter von Moos's extremely convincing argument that John's conception of logical probability as worked out in the *Metalogicon* constitutes the central intellectual foundation of the method of teaching by *exemplum* that stands at the heart of the *Policraticus*.[127] Von Moos asserts that John articulates notions of reason and logic in the *Metalogicon* that are Abelardian in character, derived from his former master's methods employed in *Sic et Non* and else-where.[128] In turn, the use of *exempla* in the *Policraticus*, which is especially no-ticeable in Books 4–6 and Book 8, chapters 17–23, constitutes a direct applica-tion of Abelard's teaching about logical probability. It is likely, indeed, that one of the reasons John felt it necessary to compose the first and second books of the *Metalogicon* so soon on the heels of completing the main body of the *Policrati-cus* may have been to elucidate (whether for himself or for potential critics) the logical premises of the latter book.

To recapitulate the proposed revised dating of John's major philosophical works:

Before mid-1157:	*Metalogicon* Book 3, Book 4.1–6 (possibly also 4.7–41)
Late 1156–mid-1157:	*Policraticus* Book 7.pro.–16, Book 7.25, Book 8.pro.–14, Book 8.24, beginning of Book 8.25
Mid-1157–late 1158:	*Policraticus* Books 1–6, Book 7.17–24, Book 8.15–23
Late-1158–late 1159:	*Metalogicon* Prologue, Books 1–2, Book 4.42
Late 1159:	*Policraticus* Prologue, end of Book 8.25

Such a chronology produces the impression of a more evenly distributed output, and compensates for times when John on his own report was particularly occu-pied with the business of Canterbury. In addition, it lends historical credence to the evident intellectual interconnections between the two texts.

While the major tasks associated with composing the *Policraticus* and the *Metalogicon* seem to have been finished by October 1159, John may have occa-sionally continued to revise or refine his texts. He would have had little time for such enterprises in the immediately ensuing period, however. Theobald grew ever more infirm over the course of the next eighteen months, and John was called upon to transact a sizeable proportion of ecclesiastical business, attested

---

[127] Peter von Moos, *Geschichte als Topik: Das rhetorische Exemplum von der Antike zur Neuzeit und die historiae im 'Policraticus' Johanns von Salisbury* (Hildesheim: Olms, 1988), 238–309.

[128] Von Moos, *Geschichte als Topik*, 266–72, 274–85.

by the large body of his correspondence in the archbishop's name dating from this time. When Theobald died on April 18, 1161, it was John who had drafted his farewell letter to Henry II, calling upon the king to choose as his successor "a lover of religion and one who may be deemed acceptable to the Most High by reason of his virtue."[129] While Theobald seems at one time to have contemplated Thomas Becket as a worthy replacement,[130] there is no great reason to suppose that after the archdeacon's disloyalty to Canterbury, the archbishop harbored any lingering desire to see this wish fulfilled. Yet it was Becket who, after a more than year's wait, came to occupy the vacant office, consecrated on June 3, 1162.

The Becket Dispute (1162–1170)

John's activities in the wake of Theobald's death again become shrouded. If he continued to work at Canterbury during the vacancy, we have no record of it. He seems to have supervised the collection of his own letters, both personal and professional, from his years under Theobald, based on rough drafts that had been retained in the Canterbury archives. Such collections of correspondence were not unusual during the time. John had in fact once asked Peter to send to him a volume containing Bernard of Clairvaux's letters.[131] Why John undertook this task is uncertain. One version of his anthology, containing only letters written for Theobald, may have been designed as a formulary or similar didactic device.[132] The full collection may have been been undertaken at the urging of his Canterbury colleagues, who were doubtless familiar with the superior literary quality of his correspondence.

John remained in the service of Canterbury after Becket's selection as archbishop, although his role seems to have been greatly diminished in contrast with his responsibilities under Theobald. John is identified among the "eruditi" of Thomas's circle enumerated by one of the new archbishop's closest advisors, Herbert of Bosham.[133] He was one of the members of the embassy to Pope Alexander III at Montpellier in July 1162 that received the archbishop's *pallium*. Upon his return to England, he compiled a brief and largely derivative life of St. Anselm,[134] apparently at the instruction of Becket, who planned to pursue the canonization of his forerunner at the Council of Tours in May 1163. It is unknown whether John played any further part in the process of preparing for the Council, which, in any case, never took up the case for Anselm's sainthood. At the age of about 45, John had in effect graduated to *emeritus* status: a symbol of continuity with the previous archbishop and a figurehead to be displayed to the world outside of Canterbury. Because John had cultivated personal relationships

---

[129] *Letters*, 1:250 (Letter 135).
[130] *Entheticus*, 188.
[131] *Letters*, 1:51 (Letter 31).
[132] *Letters*, 2:ix–x.
[133] *MB*, 3:523–31.
[134] PL 199.1009–1040.

with leading ecclesiastical (and also secular) figures throughout Europe, his "public relations" value in diplomatic matters was far greater than any other contribution he might make to Becket's *curia*. It might also be speculated that Becket did not feel entirely comfortable keeping in his immediate circle an individual who had been publicly critical in letters and writings of his own errant ways while chancellor.

The events of Becket's conflict with Henry II, his exile, and his eventual martyrdom have been recounted and scrutinized so often in literary as well as scholarly form that it seems hardly necessary to recount them.[135] John's activities during the course of the unfolding crisis within the English church were in many ways marginal to and separate from Becket's cause, which again highlights the lack of intimacy that characterized their relationship. John left England in late 1163 or early 1164—a full year before the archbishop—for reasons that remain obscure. John's letter to Becket reporting his journey to France and his contacts with various communities and lords contains ambiguities. On the one hand, John suggests that he is carrying out Thomas's instructions by meeting with Count Philip of Amiens, from whom a promise of support is extracted in the event that the archbishop is forced into exile.[136] John also visited (apparently on his own decision) King Louis VII of France seeking royal support and patronage for the cause of Canterbury. From the perspective of the letter, then, John appears to be serving as Becket's advance herald, utilizing his extensive network of political connections to offer a pro-Canterbury account of the deteriorating condition of church-state relations in England. John reminds Becket that his instructions involved making his way to Paris, renewing his ties with the schools, and doing his best to avoid suspicion that he was working as an agent of the archbishop (a plan that soon proved simply unaffordable).[137]

However, John's letter to Becket also contains the statement that "I am under the king's disfavor (undeservedly, I swear on conscience) and if I withstand his envoys, that disfavor will be greater."[138] Taken in conjunction with a later recollection by William FitzStephen, another intimate of Becket's, that John had been sent into exile by Henry II in order to prevent him from counseling the archbishop,[139] some scholars have concluded that the real reason for the departure was royal proscription.[140] Certainly, the *Policraticus*, with its lengthy discussion of tyrannicide, would hardly curry favor with Henry II, had he known of it; and John had already established his reputation at the royal court as an implacable defender of the rights of the English church and of its primate. Moreover, the incomes due to John, and to his brother Richard, who accompanied him, were eventually cut off by royal decree, but this may have been simply part of the later general prohibition following the exodus of Becket's supporters to France during the following months.

---

[135] A useful survey may be found in Barlow, *Thomas Becket*, 74–250.

[136] *Letters*, 2:2–5 (Letter 136).

[137] *Letters*, 2:10–13 (Letter 136).

[138] *Letters*, 2:12–13 (Letter 136).

[139] *MB*, 3:46.

[140] Anne Duggan, "John of Salisbury and Thomas Becket," in *WJS*, 429–30.

Two scenarios, then, seem possible. First, Becket sent John to the continent as a vanguard ambassador responsible for representing his cause and securing his base among ecclesiastical and lay lords there. Henry II heard of this and decreed that John might not return, calculating (correctly, it seems) that without access to revenue he would be unable to act effectively on the archbishop's behalf overseas. John does indeed complain to Becket that he will not be able to accomplish very much on account of his unexpectedly high expenditures during the initial phase of his travels across France.[141] The second scenario has John fleeing Henry's wrath while also taking the opportunity to serve Becket as an emissary in the ways he describes. He finds that he is less effective than hoped because of the lack of funds, and is forced to embrace a sedentary mode of life. Either arrangement of the facts withstands critical appraisal, although the former may perhaps be preferred because of John's clear implication throughout the first correspondence with the archbishop that he had consented to an extensive plan of action (an intelligence and recognizance mission, in effect) on Becket's behalf from which he has been forced to retreat by straitened financial circumstances.

John soon settled with his friend Peter of Celle, who in 1162 had been transferred to the post of abbot of St. Rémi in Rheims. It was here that John would remain in residence almost exclusively until the return of Becket's supporters to England in 1170. When Becket and his entourage arrived in France in late 1164, they sought refuge first at the Abbey of Pontigny, and later at St. Columba in Sens, both some distance from Rheims. There is no evidence that John ever remained with Thomas for any extended period, which is perhaps fortunate, since their communications were instead recorded in a body of correspondence that was eventually collected by John. Such geographic distance may also indicate John's sense of his relationship with the incumbent archbishop: he was a servant of Canterbury, not a personal aide to Becket.

The question of John's loyalty to Becket during the period of exile is a vexed one. His letters reveal an attitude of displeasure with all the main parties to the dispute: King Henry II, the English ecclesiastical hierarchy, the Canterbury curia, and Archbishop Thomas himself. John McLoughlin has proposed the highly plausible hypothesis that John's correspondence displays a decisive change in thinking about the conflict around the middle of 1166.[142] Prior to that point, John seems to regard Henry and Becket to be engaged in a largely personal quarrel between two offices (king and archbishop) that need not—indeed, ought not—embroil the whole of the English church. Henry's attacks on Thomas constituted for John a personal "tribulation" for the archbishop and "test" of his resolve. Beginning in the summer of 1166, however, John's discourse shifts decisively toward what McLoughlin terms "the language of persecution," characterized by insistent references to the passion of Christ and the Roman repression of the early church. John now views the conflict in terms of principle and

---

[141] *Letters*, 2:12–13 (Letter 136).

[142] John McLoughlin, "The Language of Persecution: John of Salisbury and the Early Phrase of the Becket Dispute," in *Persecution and Toleration*, ed. W.J. Sheils, Studies in Church History 21 (Oxford: Blackwell, 1984), 73–87.

recognizes that its resolution has implications for the whole of the English church and perhaps the organization of secular-temporal relations throughout Christendom. This is a position that Becket and his defenders had already started to enunciate in 1163, but that John was late coming to embrace.

How do we explain such a clear transformation in John's position? It may be that, on account of his early departure to England, John failed to understand the magnitude of the scheme of royal control that Henry had wished to impose upon the English church. After all, John knew both men personally, and must have recognized that they each possessed stubborn, temperamental, and single-minded characters. From a distance, their quarrel may have looked like a clash of personalities that could be settled through a greater degree of mutual understanding and compromise. As the truth about their incommensurable visions of the relationship between the spiritual and the secular spheres began to sink in, however, John found himself forced to make a choice. And his decision, flowing from his own conception of political life no less than from his professional experience, drove him to accept without qualification the side of Becket.

It is likely that a very specific event triggered John's determination: his face-to-face meeting with Henry II at the end of April or beginning of May 1166. John had been seeking such a conference for some time in the hope of making peace with the king and restoring himself to England. In a letter written during 1164 or 1165, he explains how he had attempted to chart an independent path in the conflict between Henry and Becket, supporting the archbishop "when justice and discretion seemed to be with him" but opposing him "if ever he seemed to steer away from justice or pass due measure."[143] Likewise, John says, "I have done nothing intentionally against the honor due to the king or his interests, as I am prepared to expound, if I am free to do so safely."[144] He expresses his readiness to take an oath to this effect, and also to pay whatever penalty is required of him if he is found guilty of diminishing the royal honor. John reports that discussions have commenced to restore him to royal favor,[145] but that Pope Alexander has cautioned him "to wait until the king's wrath has subsided a little." John's ambivalence toward Becket is palpable: he will do nothing to diminish the position of the archbishop, but he renounces his status as a member of the Canterbury curia. "The lord of Canterbury himself knows that I have removed myself from his household (*consortio*), but I remove neither faith nor charity."[146] John clearly believes that a separate peace with the king can be negotiated on terms that do not dishonor the cause of Canterbury.

---

[143] *Letters*, 2:22–23 (Letter 139). On the overtly Aristotelian bearing of this statement, see Cary J. Nederman, "Aristotelian Ethics and John of Salisbury's Letters," *Viator* 18 (1987): 161–73.

[144] *Letters*, 2:22–23 (Letter 139).

[145] Possibly a reference to the efforts of Peter of Celle to open channels of communication; see *Letters*, 2:30–31 (Letter 144). John also pleaded with other influential friends to intercede with the king; see *Letters*, 2:14–17 (Letter 137), 48–49 (Letter 150).

[146] *Letters*, 2:22–23 (Letter 139).

That belief shatters, however, after John meets with the king around Easter 1166. He reports that Henry demanded of him what he could not in good conscience offer, namely, that he swear an oath renouncing obedience to Becket.[147] Such a promise would have constituted a direct breach of John's own principles regarding the primacy of Canterbury in matters of faith, especially binding upon a cleric like himself. Henry, in short, wished to interfere with the good order and liberty of the English church by demanding that its servants place loyalty to the crown above fidelity to their ecclesiastical superiors. That John's experience with the king clearly demonstrated to him what was at stake in the conflict with Becket seems evident from the immediately changed tone of his correspondence, as analyzed by McLoughlin. No longer did he contemplate compromise and negotiation with Henry: the king was now in John's mind the implacable oppressor of the church, to whom opposition must be complete and unrelenting. In addition to immediately adopting the "language of persecution" identified by McLoughlin, John's letters now begin to describe Henry with reference to tyranny, a term that enjoys special significance in his political vocabulary.[148] Henry henceforth comes to be considered the sort of ruler whom it is licit to kill if the opportunity presents itself.[149]

The failure to reach accommodation in 1166 shaped the quantity as well as the quality of John's efforts on behalf of Becket. Although too poor to travel extensively, John began to put his pen (and the literary reputation behind it) to use in advocating the cause of the archbishop and defending his strategies, as well as offering him advice (albeit perhaps not always wanted). John's collection contains perhaps two dozen letters on various matters written between early 1164 and Easter 1166, including three messages to Becket. During the next four-and-a-half years, until the departure for England in November 1170, John produced nearly one hundred and fifty letters, among which seven are addressed to Becket, and nearly all of which are directly related to furthering the archbishop's position. This significant increase in output would indicate John's recognition that the king's goals were incompatible with the liberties of the English church.

The contents of the letters also give us an insight into the shift in John's attitude. Where the initial missives directed to Becket urge on him a policy of moderation and patience, the later ones are far more blunt in promoting a program aimed at defeating the king and his supporters within the church by adopting whatever measures are available.[150] John becomes more militant in his thinking. Moreover, John begins to accumulate and disseminate information helpful to negotiating the tortuous politics that swirl around the Becket conflict. If he cannot

---

[147] *Letters*, 2:84–87 (Letter 164), 94–99 (Letter 167), 198–99 (Letter 199).

[148] *Letters*, 2:427–28 (Letter 234), 434–35 (Letter 235), 580–81 (Letter 275), 614–17 (Letter 281).

[149] On John's approach to the tyrant in the *Policraticus*, see Cary J. Nederman, "A Duty to Kill: John of Salisbury's Theory of Tyrannicide," *Review of Politics* 50 (1988): 365–89.

[150] See, for instance, John's advice to Becket in July 1166 about the disposition of the English bishops who remained loyal to Henry (*Letters*, 2:172–75 [Letter 176]).

travel on the archbishop's behalf, then he can communicate and gather intelligence in that manner. Here John's rhetorical skills and noted reputation as a correspondent served him admirably. Drawing on his network of acquaintances, he filtered news from Germany and Italy, as well as France and England, about the machinations of the English crown and its allies, such as Emperor Frederick Barbarossa and the anti-popes whose claim he defended. Little wonder that John's second correspondence collection is considered an invaluable historical source not merely for the Becket dispute, but also for events of importance throughout Europe. His letters testify to his role as a sort of "clearing house" for propaganda favoring Becket as well as the flow of knowledge about the latest schemes both pro- and contra-Canterbury.

Although correspondence seems to have constituted the bulk of John's literary efforts during the later 1160s, we may date one work of a more reflective nature to the period of his residence in Rheims: the *Historia Pontificalis*. He makes no reference anywhere in his letters of the time to working on this history of the papal court and its affairs between the 1148 Council of Rheims and the early 1150s (with some sideways glances to earlier events by way of background), just as he generally does not discuss his private writing activities in his earlier correspondence. The modern editor of the *Historia Pontificalis*, Marjorie Chibnall, dates its composition on good evidence to the years of John's residence with Peter of Celle at St. Rémi, and "probably early in that period."[151] While John may have made notes or composed diaries previously concerning the events that he witnessed at the Council of Rheims, Chibnall believes that to date a significant part of the treatise to the period immediately following John's entry into Theobald's service would deny what she takes to be its internal integrity. Given what we have already observed about the ebb of John's correspondence prior to his meeting with Henry II during the spring of 1166, and its furious flow thereafter, it does not seem unreasonable to posit the main period of the work's composition between John's arrival in Rheims in early 1164 and his encounter with the king. The fact that the book is left unfinished—indeed, the text breaks off abruptly—might suggest that John turned suddenly to other business. Of course, as with his other important writings, John may have tinkered with the *Historia Pontificalis* as time and energy permitted during later years.

In view of this dating, it is entirely plausible to treat the *Historia Pontificalis* as a sort of consolation, analogous to the first-written sections of the *Policraticus*. John was, we ought not to forget, once again in disfavor with Henry II and unable to take action due to circumstances (finances, chiefly, but also the lingering wrath of the king). John comments more than once that Peter of Celle had encouraged him to write the work, and its themes have special resonance with Peter's known interests.[152] Perhaps Peter felt that the sting of Henry's disdain might be diminished a little if John were to devote his intellect to some distracting yet worthwhile pursuit such as writing. Peter was probably not present at the

---

[151] Marjorie Chibnall, "John of Salisbury as Historian," in *WJS*, 169; also see *Historia Pontificalis*, xxiv–xxx.

[152] Chibnall, "John of Salisbury as Historian," 172.

Council of Rheims; John, as mentioned previously, seems to have served as his agent there. Thus, Peter invited John to set down formally the account that had been given to him many years before of that momentous and tumultuous time. The fact that they both now resided in Rheims adds poignancy (and also immediacy) to the request. Might it be possible that John began to compose the *Historia Pontificalis* after consulting a written memorandum of events that he had presented to Peter in 1148 and that had been retained by his old friend? The evidence is entirely circumstantial, but affords an intriguing possibility.

In any case, the *Historia Pontificalis* should not be treated as a simple work of historical narrative as modern people might understand it. For John, "history" describes the facts per se, which must be "woven together" using rhetorical strategies and devices.[153] While purporting to extend previous chronicles, John uses the opportunity to ruminate about some of his favorite themes from his own prior works. As we have already seen, the *Historia Pontificalis* contains a detailed account of the trial of Gilbert of Poitiers, as well as a lengthy exposition and defense of his ideas; this discussion takes up more than a quarter of the extant text. The section concerning Gilbert supplements directly the materials on philosophy and theology found in the *Metalogicon*. Much of the remainder of the work develops John's conception of orderly government articulated in the *Policraticus* by addressing the role that the institutional church (especially the papacy) ought to play in the political realm. John O. Ward has rightly described the bulk of the *Historia Pontificalis* as concerned with "the pope in society, not the papacy, not the pope as a man."[154] Obviously, with the schism between Alexander III and the imperially-sponsored anti-popes very much on John's mind, one should hardly be surprised that he would take up this theme, refracted through the prism of an earlier time when the unity of the church had been more effectively maintained. None of this is to suggest that the *Historia Pontificalis* lacks historical value, but it should not be regarded as primarily a work of history in a modern, or perhaps even a medieval, sense.

Final Years (1171–1180)

The restoration of Becket to residence at Canterbury resulted from a prolonged set of negotiations in which John seems to have played a relatively minor role. He traveled in 1167 and again in 1169 to conduct meetings with papal legates charged with resolving the dispute.[155] In February 1170, he may also have journeyed to Pontoise to attend a conference between Becket and Henry II that was ultimately cancelled. John gives a narration of the events in a letter to Archdea-

---

[153] John O. Ward, "Some Principles of Rhetorical Historiography in the Twelfth Century," in *Classical Rhetoric and Medieval Historiography*, ed. Ernst Breisach (Kalamazoo: Medieval Institute, 1985), 103–65, here 107–8.

[154] Ward, "Some Principles of Rhetorical Historiography," 109.

[155] *Letters*, 2:406–23 (Letters 230–231), 660–63 (Letter 290).

con Baldwin of Totnes, but does not specifically identify himself as present.[156] By 1169, it is clear that both Becket and Henry were under a great deal of pressure from both ecclesiastical and temporal lords throughout Europe to reach a settlement on what had become a somewhat embarrassing episode in the history of church-state relations. Yet each, for his own reasons, refused to yield. Only on July 22, 1170 was an agreement reached, permitting the archbishop and those in exile with him to return to their offices and lands in England.

John was assigned to head a transition team to prepare Becket's return and he crossed the English Channel in mid-November. Writing to Peter of Celle several weeks later, he reports that he found the situation in confusion. Rights and goods that were to be returned to the jurisdiction of Canterbury remained in the hands of royal officials. Meanwhile, John as appointed representative of the archbishop received neither cooperation nor respect from the king's men. Even the return of Thomas himself in December did nothing to improve circumstances; the king seems to have violated the terms of the agreement and returned to his old ways of bullying and interfering with the business of the archbishop. By contrast, John's life as an exile at St. Rémi now appears to him "the likeness of paradise."[157]

Then on December 29 occurred the fated and fabled murder of Becket in Canterbury Cathedral. John was present in conference with the archbishop when the knights of Henry's court arrived to confront their nemesis. For all the narration based on eyewitness accounts, the events of that day remain blurred. In one of his most famous letters to the bishop of Poitiers, John of Canterbury, John gives an almost instantaneous report of the martyrdom, but it is by no means based entirely on first-hand knowledge.[158] In spite of the claim by one assassin that his sword had wounded the arm of John of Salisbury, this identification is mistaken; he actually attacked another associate of Becket, the monk Edward Grim. John instead fled the scene of the ambush along with most of the other members of the archbishop's group, hiding elsewhere in the cathedral. What the letter to John of Canterbury makes clear is the status of Becket as a saint-in-waiting who had begun to perform miracles immediately following his death. Thus, John instantly took a leading role in promoting the cult of Thomas Becket. This was a cause to which he would devote much energy, not least in the hopes of furthering the hegemony of Canterbury over the English church and the independence of that church from the crown, two of his favorite ambitions.

The evidence for John's waning years is almost as sketchy and imprecise as for his youth. We know for certain that he received two ecclesiastical preferments during the 1170s. He was made Treasurer of Exeter in 1173 and was consecrated bishop of Chartres in August 1176. These offices must have finally given John some relief from the complaints of poverty that had dogged him from his days in Paris throughout his career under Theobald and Becket. But even in a late letter to Peter of Celle, he carps about the frailty of his material

---

[156] *Letters*, 2:690–97 (Letter 298).

[157] *Letters*, 2:714–25 (Letter 304).

[158] *Letters*, 2:725–37 (Letter 305).

circumstances, perhaps due to the Great Rebellion of 1173, although the main battles do not seem to have unduly affected the south of England in either the east or the west.[159]

John's positions at Exeter and then Chartres reaffirmed his long-standing network of associations. Both the bishop and archdeacon of Exeter were old friends with whom John communicated regularly during the Becket crisis; he had received a significant portion of his education in the town as well, and thus he seems to have been a figure well known to the chapter. There is reason to suppose that John gravitated after the death of Becket more toward Devon than Kent.[160] He continued to have some involvement in the affairs of Canterbury, such as promoting the confirmation and consecration of the successor to Becket, Prior Richard of Dover, but even this activity seems to have been undertaken for the most part from afar.[161]

The years immediately following the assassination of Becket occasioned John's last flurry of literary activity: the composition of a hagiography of Thomas and the compilation of the second correspondence collection covering the years 1164 to 1170. The history of these two projects appears to be entangled in great measure, and so the sequence has been difficult to establish. The work in particular of Christopher Brooke and Anne Duggan, however, has done much to clarify our understanding.[162] During his idle hours at Exeter, John seems to have commenced work on an edition of his own letters pertaining in particular to the Becket dispute and its aftermath. The ascription of this collection to the time spent in Devon derives mainly from the fact that he employs copies of correspondence that had been addressed to Archbishop Bartholomew and from the inclusion in the volume of some late letters drafted by John for the archbishop's signature. Since the letters fall off to a trickle after 1173, it seems reasonable to date the bulk of the work on this edition to that year or the next.

Quite possibly during the same period, on those occasions when John was in residence at Canterbury, he undertook, with the assistance of Guy of Southwick, a canon of Merton, to collect a number of letters—his own and others—directly related to Becket's conflict with Henry and the martyrdom. He prefaced this work with a short and hastily written account of Thomas's life and death, which was itself heavily dependent upon several other sources, including already circulating hagiographies and his own account in the letter to John of Canterbury of the actual murder. There has been considerable confusion about the relationship between this volume (now lost) and the edition of letters concerning Becket compiled by Alan of Tewkesbury, which is prefaced by John's *Vita et Passio Sancti Thome* in a version that is heavily supplemented by Alan. The

[159] *Letters*, 2:754–61 (Letter 310); see Warren, *Henry II*, 123, 129–31.
[160] *Letters*, 2:xlvi.
[161] *Letters*, 2:766–85 (Letters 312–321).
[162] *Letters*, 2:xlvi–lxiii; Anne J. Duggan, *Thomas Becket: A Textual History of His Letters* (Oxford: Clarendon Press, 1980), 85–90, 94–98; eadem, ed., *The Correspondence of Thomas Becket Archbishop of Canterbury 1162–1170*, 2 vols. (Oxford: Clarendon Press, 2000), 1:xxi–lxviii.

former work, the contents of which are known through a *florilegium* by Guy, seems to have much in common with the latter in terms of organization. The quite plausible suggestion of Duggan and Brooke is that John worked with Guy on the enterprise as time permitted, composing his life of Thomas as an intro-duction to the collection. But he abandoned the edition and handed it over to Alan of Tewkesbury for completion. The reason for this, Brooke surmises, was John's sudden and unexpected transfer in 1176 to Chartres, where he was unlikely to enjoy access to the materials required to finish his work. There is some small independent evidence that Alan took up this project immediately and that the collection was finished very late in 1176 or in 1177. How far along it was when John passed it over to Alan remains unknown, but the testimony of Guy's *florilegium* suggests that its arrangement at least was largely settled.

In light of his lengthy history of contention with Henry II, John was unlikely to receive high ecclesiastical office in England or in any continental territories under Plantagenet control. His chances elsewhere, by contrast, proved much better. John's election to Chartres may be attributed to the connections he cultivated with the spiritual and temporal authorities in France during his years of exile (and not, as was long surmised, the result of his youthful association with a "School of Chartres"). At the behest of both his predecessor, William "White Hands" (who had resigned in order to become archbishop of Rheims), and King Louis VII, the chapter at Chartres chose him expressly in honor of St. Thomas of Canterbury. Since it was exceptional for someone from a family out-side the king's circle—and a foreigner at that—to be elected to a royal bishop-ric,[163] the political situation leading to John's selection may require some com-ment.[164] William "White Hands" was descended from one of the most brilliant families of northern France—great-grandson of William the Conqueror, nephew of King Stephen, brother of Count Henry (the Liberal) of Champagne and Count Theobald IV of Blois, and brother-in-law of King Louis. Throughout the Becket conflict, he played an important role as mediator and negotiator, but was clearly someone who favored Canterbury's cause. At the time William resigned Char-tres, he was a pluralist, holding in addition the office of Archbishop of Sens, which he also surrendered. Chartres itself was Count Theobald's town, but the bishopric was the king's to bestow. This is obviously why White Hands was a natural incumbent—with family connections on both sides—but his pluralism doubtless stirred no end of grumbling. As a purely political matter, John of Salisbury made a very attractive choice: a man well known to King Louis, and

---

[163] See Elizabeth M. Hallam, *Capetian France 987–1328* (London: Longman, 1980), 195–96; and Marcel Pacaut, *Les Elections épiscopales dans l'église de France du IXe au XIIe siècle* (Paris: Vrin, 1957), 105.

[164] For the following, I am greatly indebted to Christopher Crockett, a lifelong spe-cialist in twelfth-century Chartrean history, with whom I have for many years profitably corresponded about these matters. In particular, I appreciate his sharing with me a me-ticulously annotated (by him) charter of c. 1178 resolving a dispute over a house and vineyard illegally built in the woods of Nottonville controlled by the monastery of Mar-moutier (H.2369/3: 1178).

one for whom Archbishop William could also vouch to his family. Moreover, as a very senior person unlikely to be seeking further preferment, while at the same time an inexperienced leader, John was likely to defer to the interests and wishes of those who had arranged his election. While we know nothing further of the circumstances of his elevation, there must have been significant maneuvering and maybe compromise during the process, about which John perhaps knew little.

Any definitive evaluation of the strengths and weaknesses of John's term as archbishop must await a careful culling of the archives for an edition of his acts and charters that does not yet exist.[165] The years of his episcopacy do not seem in any case to have been strenuous ones in the ecclesiastical politics of the see. The charters ascribed to him tend to be purely judicial instruments (unlike in earlier times), dry and formula-laden. There are not many extant letters dating to the period on which to form a judgment. From two missives dating to 1180, we know that he had excommunicated John, count of Vendôme, soon after his consecration, supposedly for trampling the rights of a religious house in his county.[166] But the events leading up to the excommunication almost certainly antedated John's accession and it seems likely that the new bishop was merely confirming the wishes of his powerful predecessor. Among John's other activities while serving at Chartres that can be determined for certain were his witnessing of the treaty of Ivry in September 1177 between Kings Louis VII and Henry II committing them to a plan of crusade (eventually aborted) and otherwise resolving outstanding differences between them; and his attendance at the Third Lateran Council where he was commissioned as an appellate judge on behalf of Pope Alexander to consider a difficult case from England.[167]

The more subjective elements of John's episcopal career are harder to assess. On the one hand, as Beryl Smalley points out, the evaluation contained in his official necrology is substantially positive. He is depicted there as "a learned and lovable pastor" who gained for his see the right to manumit its serfs without prior secular approval and to appeal to witness rather than ordeal as a basis for proof in judicial proceedings.[168] Of course, such necrologies tended to be extremely laudatory, so perhaps nothing can be gleaned from this one. On the other hand, Egbert Türk concludes from two letters by Peter of Celle and one by Peter of Blois that John permitted himself to become ensnared in the frivolities of courtiers that he so abhorred.[169] Peter chastises John for his faithlessness as a correspondent and rumors of ingratitude toward those who have looked after

[165] *Letters*, 2:809.

[166] The letters are published by J. A. Giles, ed., *Joannis Saresberiensis Opera Omnia*, v. 2 (Oxford: J. H. Parker, 1848), 294–96.

[167] See Warren, Henry II, 145–47; Jan van Laarhoven, "Non iam decreta, sed Evangelium! Jean de Salisbury au Latran III," in *Dalla Chiesa antica alla Chiesa moderna: Miscellanea per il Cinquantesimo della Facoltà di Storia Ecclesiastica della Pontificia Università Gregoriana,* ed. Mario Fois, Vincenzo Monachino, and Felix Litva (Rome: Pontifical Gregorian University, 1987), 107–19.

[168] Smalley, *The Becket Conflict and the Schools*, 107–8.

[169] Türk, *Nugae Curialium*, 93–94.

him. What can be inferred from this is doubtful, since John and Peter employed *topoi* of apology for and teasing admonition about inconstancy throughout their personal correspondence over several decades. The letter from Peter of Blois is more serious. Peter charges that a faction of canons had blocked his already accomplished selection as provost of Chartres in favor of John's own nephew, Robert. This is the only reference to a nephew named Robert, and the list of Chartrean provosts from that time (which may, admittedly, be incomplete) does not include anyone named Robert.[170] What we make of this letter, with its apparent charge of nepotism, or at least favoritism, depends upon the existence of additional evidence that is not presently available. Türk's conclusion that John was incapable of improving upon his fellow courtiers when handed the reins of power seems, at any rate, unsupported by the letters in question.

John's death is recorded on October 25, 1180 at an age of sixty or more. He was to be succeeded at Chartres by his old friend Peter of Celle, who was also to die in this office. John is buried in the Lady Chapel of the Abbey of Josaphat de Lèves near Chartres, where his tomb and epitaph may be observed today. To the cathedral chapter of Chartres he bequeathed all his worldly goods, including vestments and a relic of St. Thomas of Canterbury (a vial of the saint's blood), as well as a substantial personal library containing a complete Bible, scriptural commentaries, patristic works, and a number of pagan classics, in addition to a copy of the *Policraticus*.[171] Before the Second World War, Clement Webb examined the medieval manuscripts extant in the Bibliothèque Municipale in Chartres, which houses the remains of the chapter library. He was able to identify four manuscripts that may have formed part of John's library.[172] More recently, Lynn Barker has established the probability that a manuscript of Lactantius's *Institutiones Divinae* presently owned by the Bodleian had been part of John's bequest to Chartres.[173] John's private library in a very significant way reflected the man: religious yet humanistic, eclectic in intellect yet respectful of tradition and authority. These qualities always marked his writings as much as his life and career.

---

[170] I am grateful to a private correspondence from Christopher Crockett dated June 16, 1992 for this information, which he derived from a chronological list of Chartrean office-holders edited by archivist Lucien Merlet and published by his son, René, in 1900.

[171] A complete inventory with comments is given by Clement C. J. Webb, *John of Salisbury* (London: Methuen, 1932), 165–68.

[172] Clement C. J. Webb, "Note on Books Bequeathed by John of Salisbury to the Cathedral Library of Chartres," *Medieval and Renaissance Studies* 1 (1943): 128–29.

[173] Lynn K. Barker, "MS Bodl. Canon. Pat. Lat. 131 and a Lost Lactantius of John of Salisbury: Evidence in Search of a French Critic of Thomas Becket," *Albion* 22 (1990): 21–37.

CHAPTER TWO

WRITINGS

"Humanism" is the term that has customarily been reserved to characterize the thought of John of Salisbury. John has indeed been proclaimed the quintessential figure of twelfth-century humanism. But the very idea of medieval humanism is fraught with problems, as even its leading scholars realize. To call John a humanist, then, only begs the question: what sort of humanist *was* he?

One answer to this question, expounded most influentially by Hans Liebeschütz, associates John's thought with the so-called "literary" humanism that typified the quattrocento Renaissance.[1] This approach concentrates upon the nature and extent of his classical learning, as well as the manner in which he applied the wisdom of the ancients. Liebeschütz thus often judges John's ideas on the basis of their fidelity to classical sources.[2] We now know, of course, that John's apparent familiarity with the classics cannot be taken at face value.[3] More importantly, as Richard Southern has insisted, his intent in reading classical authorities differed greatly from that of the humanists of later times: "John of Salisbury was motivated by a strong desire to get from all the ancient texts at his disposal their maximum contribution to doctrine, quite regardless of the literary aims of the works in which these choice fragments of general truth were embedded."[4] John was simply too enmeshed in the quest for specifically Christian knowledge in matters natural as well as supernatural to defer to the study of classical language and literature on its own terms.

Southern and others have emphasized a different narrative of medieval humanism that stresses its Christian and scholastic bases.[5] According to this view,

---

[1] Hans Liebeschütz, *Mediaeval Humanism in the Life and Writings of John of Salisbury* (London: The Warburg Institute, 1950), 1–7. The roots of this position can be traced at least as far back as Charles Homer Haskins, *The Renaissance of the Twelfth Century* (Cambridge, MA: Harvard University Press, 1927), for whom the study of the classics was a "barometer" for the general level of intellectual activity. On this, see Marcia L. Colish, *Remapping Scholasticism*, The Etienne Gilson Series 21 (Toronto: Pontifical Institute of Medieval Studies, 2000), 2–5.

[2] Liebeschütz, *Mediaeval Humanism in the Life and Writings of John of Salisbury*, 63–90.

[3] See Janet Martin, "John of Salisbury as Classical Scholar," in *WJS*, 179–201.

[4] R. W. Southern, *Scholastic Humanism and the Unification of Europe*, v. 1 (Oxford: Blackwell, 1995), 19.

[5] In addition to Southern, *Scholastic Humanism and the Unification of Europe*, 1:17–45, see idem, *Medieval Humanism and Other Essays* (Oxford: Blackwell, 1970), 29–60 and C. Stephen Jaeger, *Medieval Humanism in Gottfried von Strassburg's Tristan und Isolde* (Heidelberg: Carl Winter, 1977) and *The Envy of Angels: Cathedral Schools and Social Ideals in Medieval Europe, 950–1250* (Philadelphia: University of Pennsylvania

the humanist elements in John's thought derive from a recognition of human dignity and of the concomitant dignity of nature, both of which are intelligible and may be accessed by human beings through the application of reason.[6] The truth that John seeks is hence nothing less than a comprehensive knowledge of the operation of the universe in which humanity itself constitutes the noblest (if still flawed, because fallen) of God's creations. Humanism embraces an optimistic confidence that the acquisition of such truth about divine creation is not only possible but in addition constitutes a demonstration of religious devotion. This definition of humanism, however, also fails to capture important features of John's thinking, notably his skepticism and his activism. Throughout his writings, John professes to follow the moderate skepticism of the New Academy, and protests that the human mind is poorly equipped to know very much with certainty. The best we can hope for, he says, is probable truth, always subject to reevaluation and revision. The powers of human reason—its ability to intuit the cosmos and humanity's place therein—are modest in comparison with the claims made for John's humanism. Furthermore, it must not be overlooked that John in his maturity was never mainly or essentially a scholar. His was a life of action, not reflection. Indeed, he often stated that the life of the mind and the active life were mutually reinforcing. It is clear from John's biography that he took care to follow the footprints of philosophers in his conduct of public affairs, but at the same time to let experience and a certain pragmatism guide his intellectual pursuits. While he often complained about the distractions of the court drawing him away from reading and writing, this *topos* dates at least as far back as his hero Cicero. The "scholastic humanism" posited by Southern does not fully address the active and practical dimensions of John's thought.

Must we reject, then, any effort to characterize John's ideas as "humanist" in a meaningful or useful way? One might argue that the classification of humanism has applicability to his thinking as a way of distinguishing "his great interest in things human" from "the most despairing and world-fleeing of Christians."[7] Such a minimalist definition of humanism is consonant with John's own profound Christian faith and his belief in the centrality of God to human life. The limitation of this conception of humanism, however, stems from its entirely formal and negative connotations, since it derives meaning purely in contrast to an otherworldly anti-humanism that denigrates the value of all earthly human achievements. Assuredly, John was a Christian-centered author. But just as assuredly, John believed that works of virtue and intellect could be found even among those who had not accepted (or lived before the time of) Christianity.

Therefore, we ought to determine whether John's humanism incorporates some principle that captures a more positive and substantive vision of the worthiness of humanity per se. I propose to adapt to John's case a definition offered

---

Press, 1994), esp. 278–91.

[6] Southern, *Medieval Humanism*, 31–32.

[7] Glenn W. Olsen, "John of Salisbury's Humanism," in *Gli Umanesimi Medievali*, ed. Claudio Leonardi (Florence: SISMEL, Edizioni del Galluzzo, 1998), 447–68, here 467.

many years ago: "Humanism" may be understood as "the idea that a human be-ing is meant to achieve, during life, a fair measure of human happiness. It im-plies, of course, that happiness is to be sought in a human way."[8] This definition, while concrete, is surprisingly capacious. It acknowledges that there is a human path to happiness that is sought and may be known by all human beings. Yet there is no assumption that all of humanity is happy or has attained knowledge of the proper route to becoming so; rather, the *possibility* of earthly happiness is held out to those who sincerely struggle and overcome the obstacles to its reali-zation. Happiness is not given to the human race, but is something that must be earned by exertion. And human beings can be fooled or mistaken about the cor-rect sources of happiness, for example, by confusing pleasure with true satisfac-tion. The keys to such happiness for John are discovered by following "the foot-prints of the philosophers," whose lessons give us some insight into how wisdom and virtue may be attained in the present life. Hence, the happy human existence embraces both active and reflective dimensions: one must do the good (virtue) as well as know the good (wisdom) in order to flourish.

While consistent with Christianity, a definition of humanism with reference to happiness constitutes more than a mirror opposite of Christian ascetic anti-humanism.[9] It admits that while non-Christians are unable to achieve salvation, their earthly lives may still have merit. Moreover, it means that in matters of happiness pertaining to the present life, we may learn equally from the deeds and writings of infidels as from those of believers. John's Christian humanism may thus be construed as embracing a "parallelism" in matters of instruction. Christian authorities will certainly guide us toward happiness (eternal as well as temporal), but they may usefully be supplemented by studying the acts and ideas of worthy pagans, which also contribute to instilling in humanity the virtue and wisdom that produce the measure of earthly fulfillment of which we are capable. Such themes run throughout John's writings, shaping the balance and nuance of his views. Earthly happiness is a worthy pursuit, although it is not easy to achieve. It is important to educate oneself about the obstacles that prevent hap-piness from being attained so that thereby one may be prepared to discern what is necessary and useful to becoming a truly happy person. Success is not certain, but it will never be achieved without effort. These teachings compose the core of John's version of humanism.

Entheticus de Dogmate Philosophorum

Many of the salient elements of John's humanistic perspective are already ap-parent in the *Entheticus de Dogmate Philosophorum* (*Entheticus Maior*), which comprises what seems to be his earliest known work. The title has no literal translation, containing one of the pseudo-Greek neologisms ("Entheticus") that

---

[8] Gerald G. Walsh, *Medieval Humanism* (New York: Macmillan Co., 1942), 1. Walsh derives this definition from the work of Charles Trinkaus on the Renaissance.

[9] Walsh, *Medieval Humanism*, 2–3.

were in favor among twelfth-century authors. (John employs similar neologisms as the titles of his two major philosophical works, the *Policraticus* and the *Metalogicon*.) Loosely, it might be rendered "Introduction to the Teachings of the Philosophers." A Latin poem running to 1852 lines, its purposes are both didactic and satirical. The *Entheticus Maior* instructs the reader about the sources of philosophical wisdom and virtue, the relationship between human reason and divine truth, and the good order of the school and the court. It also contains a number of scathing caricatures of the personalities whom John encountered both in the Parisian classrooms and at European courts. Modern editors have divided the *Entheticus Maior* into a prologue and four distinct parts. The prologue is brief, a mere 24 lines. The parts may be grouped together into two sections: Parts I and II, concerning the world of the schools, total 1250 lines; the Parts III and IV, which survey life at court, are much shorter, running to 578 lines. As was proposed in the biographical portion of the present study, John probably wrote the first major section of the *Entheticus Maior* while a student at Paris in the 1140s. The remainder of the poem seems to date to the middle of the 1150s, most likely before the end of 1156. It is addressed explicitly to a member of the Canterbury circle (almost certainly Thomas Becket) who has gone off to serve at the royal court.

In spite of the fragmented history of its composition, there are features of the *Entheticus Maior* that mark it with internal coherence and integrity. John employs, for example, a unifying stylistic thread, stemming from a technique pioneered by Ovid called *prosopopeia*, through which the author addresses his book as though it were a person. As van Laarhoven remarks, the *prosopopeia* "provided a good way for an author to shield himself behind such a conversation with his brain-child, whilst the identity of the true addressee is kept uncertain, being mentioned at the most by allusions."[10] When John speaks to his book, giving it instructions and guidance, his words are meant for its addressee, presumably Becket. Thus, when the book is told "be mindful of yourself,"[11] its author employs a piece of advice that echoes what he has already remarked to Becket more directly (and what he would again propose to the chancellor in other writings).[12] More overtly still, John lectures his text: "Canterbury, parent of bishops and kings, has fostered you and prepares a hospice for you, indeed a home. She asks that you return and rest in that seat which is the head of the kingdom and the home of justice. You must obey a mother who admonishes rectitude in particular, and who seeks to extend your days."[13] When read in con-

---

[10] John of Salisbury, *Entheticus Maior and Minor*, 3 vols., ed. Jan van Laarhoven (hereafter *Entheticus*) (Leiden: Brill, 1986), 1:48.

[11] *Entheticus*, 1:226–27.

[12] *Entheticus*, 1:202–3; cf. 2:423.

[13] *Entheticus*, 1:210–11. Since the poetic elements of the text are difficult to capture in English—as van Laarhoven's translation testifies—I have here and below simply rendered them in prose form, the easier to grasp the substance of John's thought. This follows the policy adopted by Ronald E. Pepin in his translation of the *Entheticus Maior* in *Allegorica* 9 (1987): 7–133.

junction with a preceding statement that Becket was Theobald's heir apparent,[14] John's application of the *prosopopeia* technique in this passage is especially transparent. It becomes impossible to distinguish between the identities of the poem and the chancellor.

A second connecting thread within the *Entheticus Maior* is its recurrent use of the motif of the journey. This aspect is closely related to the *prosopopeia* device, insofar as John couches much of his advice to his book in terms of guidance to a traveler. In particular, John recommends to his poem the safest modes of conduct while away from home and warns it about the dangers of both the trip and the destination. The travel theme is introduced almost immediately in the prologue: "The court rejoices in new friends, disdains old ones, only the cause of pleasure and profit pleases. Who are you who comes? What is the reason for the journey? Where do you go? And for what reason? Perhaps it will be asked. Respond briefly, little book."[15] The response suggested by John forms the bridge from the prologue to the doctrines of truth and virtue that form the substance of Parts I and II. In Parts III and IV, written with the court and its new denizen especially in mind, the *viator* motif returns. John first explains to the poem what perils await it amongst courtiers, counseling it in particular not to speak indiscriminately or rashly: "Either be utterly silent or speak little at court, or find out in what faraway land you can hide; for if you do not spare your words, no one will spare you, and the impious crowd will overtake your days."[16] Dissemblance is promoted as the best course of action for the *Entheticus Maior* until it can have a private word with its "patron" (who is also engaging in pious dissimulation) and return home to Canterbury. But the journey back will itself be fraught with the temptations of the flesh, which take particular root in those who frequent inns and roadhouses.[17] The safest place is back home among likeminded men of virtue and wisdom—cloistered but preferably not cowled.[18] Although not even the monastery is entirely free of "bad types," it is still more conducive to the health of the soul than any secular court. Finally, having summarized his advice for a safe trip, John sets his poem on its way: "But why do I delay any more? You are anxious to go. Watch out, what you may do; cautiously complete the journey once started."[19] From virtually beginning to end, the book is portrayed as preparing for its journey. It awaits only John's final instructions before its departure.

The convergence of the *prosopopeia* technique with the *viator* motif helps to define the purpose and dating of the *Entheticus Maior*. If the book stands in for the chancellor as the recipient of John's advice, and if that counsel is couched as guidance for the uninitiated traveler to court, then the impression is reinforced that he completed the poem soon after Thomas's departure for court.

---

[14] *Entheticus*, 1:188–89.
[15] *Entheticus*, 1:104–5.
[16] *Entheticus*, 1:202–3.
[17] *Entheticus*, 1:204–9.
[18] *Entheticus*, 1:210–11.
[19] *Entheticus*, 1:226–27.

Indeed, we might speculate that the *Entheticus Maior* was a sort of parting gift to Becket: John was warning Thomas about how to behave at court so as to advance Canterbury's interests, while reminding him that his "true home" was back in the archbishop's household. The poem was thus following in its patron's footsteps (one of John's favorite metaphors) along the route to court, but was also mapping out the path for the return journey to Canterbury (possibly as Theobald's successor). The *Entheticus Maior* reads as a travel guidebook to the alien world of secular political affairs and a reminder to Becket that he was not ultimately a member of the temporal realm but instead belonged in the spiritual sphere. That Thomas did not heed this advice, rather preferring to plunge headlong into the corruption of courtly life, perhaps points to John's sensitivity toward the flaws in his colleague's character.

The immediately practical thrust of the satirical counsel contained in the *Entheticus Maior* should not lead us to discount it as a work of intellectual significance. John's ultimate point, after all, was the entirely serious one of demonstrating to Becket the philosophical and religious principles that ought to guide his conduct as a new courtier. The prologue advises its reader to locate and converse with only those men who are true "friends of God," identifiable by their devotion to truth and virtue.[20] But how ought one to speak in the company of such persons? And how are they to be discovered among the many who feign goodness and wisdom? These questions lead John to weave into the poem a series of lessons (comprising Parts I and II) about wise and virtuous doctrine found in Christian and pagan sources alike—sections that, as already discussed, were probably composed originally during the 1140s. In the context of the broader aims of the *Entheticus Maior*, Part I has a double purpose: to explain the sources and consequences of intellectual error and to identify the basic purpose and organization of genuine learning. Grasping these lessons, John believes, renders the courtier impervious to the snares and temptations of courtly life by shaping his character in conformity with truth and virtue.

Part I opens with an expression of concern about how easy it is to be fooled by men who have been educated in the schools, since they often possess merely superficial, glib, and clever minds. John explains that their false ideas result directly from the quality of the instruction that they have received. Too commonly the schools are populated with teachers who pass off the doctrines of great thinkers—recent and ancient alike—as their own inventions. They strive for innovation, yet lack the intellectual sophistication of those authorities whom they ignore or dismiss. These masters believe (incorrectly) that their honor and status is diminished if they defer to any philosopher of the past, let alone to someone who numbers among their contemporaries.[21] Furthermore, students are encouraged to suppose that an education can be obtained without dedication and diligence. Reading, study, and assiduous practice are disdained as unnecessary to the acquisition of a learned demeanor. "Read little in order that you know much" has become a common scholastic refrain, John observes, since exposure

---

[20] *Entheticus*, 1:104–5.
[21] *Entheticus*, 1:106–9.

to many points of view produces only confusion and uncertainty.[22] The "successful" student instead tailors his learning to the ends of selfish utility, namely, wealth and glory. John laments how education has come to be considered an investment, a commodity useful in furthering the student's (and his family's) quest for position and material reward. And teachers encourage such attitudes in order to advance their own ambitions and fulfill their purposes. Real instruction is "too great a nuisance (*molesta*)" that may be dispensed with, inasmuch as the students desire to learn as little as the teacher wishes to educate. Such a bargain may be financially profitable for pupil and master alike, but it yields only the veneer of erudition and false credentials.[23] It is noteworthy that John's major object of ridicule in the *Entheticus Maior* is the flaunting of the principles of grammar (unlike in the later *Metalogicon*, in which rhetoric and dialectic are primarily defended).[24] This fact reinforces the impression that the verses comprising Part I were originally composed as an academic exercise for a course in grammar. But it also highlights John's belief that confused language and confused thinking are intimately related: those who do not write and speak coherently are not capable of attaining the knowledge necessary for virtue and wisdom. One must always be on guard for people who speak fluidly yet who say nothing, for this skill is one that the schools too often generate and indeed commend.

The only solution to the problem of empty speech, according to John, is the marriage of "Mercury" and "Philology," that is, the cultivation of real eloquence: "Mercury is the symbol for word, Philology for reason; Philosophy orders these to be joined."[25] The person whose speech is worthy of attention, then, is one who possesses the wisdom to express only those thoughts that he considers to be true (or at any rate probable) and conducive to virtue. The true philosopher—who alone is to be sought by the newly arrived courtier—is an amalgam of persuasive argumentation and wise reflection, neither silent nor boisterous, neither arrogant nor entirely self-effacing. The philosophical man is the embodiment in word and deed of the decorum praised by Cicero and other classical thinkers, an adherent always and in all things to the Aristotelian principle of the golden mean. Praise for the social ideal of the decorous philosopher is spread throughout the *Entheticus Maior*, and it becomes one of the salient doctrines of John's later writing as well. One might even say that John was immoderate in his praise of moderation as the basis for a happy and ordered human life.

Clearly, the genuine philosopher must nourish his native talents by hard work and regular study.[26] To supplement and complete his education, however, he requires grace. John upholds the position that philosophy and faith, so far from conflicting or contradicting in their truths, point to the same lessons in matters of knowledge and morals. "If the true God is the true wisdom of mankind,"

---

[22] *Entheticus*, 1:110–11.

[23] *Entheticus*, 1:112–13.

[24] *Entheticus*, 1:108–9, 114–17.

[25] *Entheticus*, 1:118–19.

[26] *Entheticus*, 1:128–29.

he remarks, "then Philosophy is love of the true God."[27] Hence John promotes a specifically Christian vision of philosophy: it remains forever in the service of and deferential to the ends of religion, because whatever wisdom one is able to attain is ultimately due to a divine gift. In particular, John's emphasis on grace as the capstone of philosophical learning has the effect of diminishing the pridefulness to which purely secular philosophy is prone.[28] The individual who maintains that his certain knowledge is wholly the result of his own talents and efforts soon falls to the temptation to raise himself above his fellow creatures and to proclaim that his superiority qualifies him for special treatment or status. Mindfulness of the role of divine grace in bestowing wisdom tempers such arrogance by restoring the discoveries of philosophical inquiry to proper perspective. Philosophy teaches us much, but it can never replace the study of holy scripture, "the queen of writings."[29] The true philosopher exercises a measure of modesty in comparing the sort of knowledge he inculcates with the higher truths taught directly by God.

Once we have recognized the place of philosophy within the scheme of human existence, John believes that we may begin to understand and judge the strengths and limitations of the ancient philosophical schools and systems. The light of reason, lit by the love of God and sheltered by the admission of its own frailties, provides the most adequate source of intellectual illumination.[30] Part II of the *Entheticus Maior* takes up the project of surveying critically the major doctrines of classical antiquity, concentrating in particular on their ideas of the *summum bonum* for humanity. In each case, John holds that the ancients grasped some aspect of the truth, yet failed to capture the full picture. The Stoics, for instance, realized that a moderate fear of death was necessary to banish evil and remind humanity of the vanity of worldly goods. Yet they incorrectly embraced a doctrine of impersonal fate that condemned the human race to an erroneous fatalism.[31] The Peripatetic followers of Aristotle, to cite another example, properly held that the power of reason permitted human beings to achieve considerable understanding of the operations of physical nature and the causal structure of the universe. At the same time, they failed to identify God as the first cause and prime mover, while their devout naturalism led them away from the *contemptus mundi* that marks the road to salvation.[32] Only the Epicurean School seems to have no redeeming value for John, inasmuch as it associates the human good with carnal pleasures.[33] John's knowledge of the classical philosophers is, admittedly, partial. His accounts of Socrates, Pythagoras, and Anaxagoras are vague and not especially insightful; of Plato, he knows mainly the later cosmological teachings contained in the *Timaeus*; Aristotle is praised for his system-

---

[27] *Entheticus*, 1:124–25.
[28] *Entheticus*, 1:150–53.
[29] *Entheticus*, 1:134–35.
[30] *Entheticus*, 1:146–49.
[31] *Entheticus*, 1:134–39.
[32] *Entheticus*, 1:144–51.
[33] *Entheticus*, 1:140–43.

atic approach to philosophical investigation, but little is said about the substance of his thought.[34] Among Hellenistic and Roman schools and authorities, John singles out for extended comment the skepticism of the later Academy and the ideas of Cicero; the former is lauded when it keeps its doubt within the bounds of moderation, while the latter is heralded not only for his eloquence but also for his teaching about the nature of divinity (presumably on the basis of a reading of *De natura deorum*).[35] Yet John does not—unlike in his later writings—label himself an adherent of the New Academy nor a devotee of Cicero. Indeed, Cicero is derided for his inability to conduct his life in complete accordance with the doctrines he espoused. John's expression of this view gives the impression of an author whose idealism suggests the short patience for compromise that signals limited experience of the world at large (perhaps another indication of an early date of the passage's composition).

At the beginning of Part III, John switches his focus from the classroom to the court, the denizens of which he pointedly rebukes for their moral impurity and intellectual vacuity. But the new courtier, affirmed in his faith, must ignore them, since he has a more pressing enterprise in which he must engage: the cancellation (a pun on "cancellarius," chancellor) of the unjust decrees that had been imposed by the prior kings of England.[36] The third and fourth parts of the *Entheticus Maior* combine biting satire with sharp political and social criticism. Yet John also acknowledges the moral complexity and ambiguity of courtly business, and avers that the well-intentioned courtier must at times adopt the tricks of his surroundings in order to survive and pursue his program of reform. The change in attitude from Part II is striking, perhaps indicative of the perspective of someone who has become familiar with the ethical dilemmas endemic to public life.

While employing pseudonyms, John primarily targets the ravages that afflicted England during the reign of King Stephen ("Hircanus"), induced by the ruler himself as well as by some of his leading courtiers ("Mandroger," "Antipater") who have oppressed the legitimate liberties of the country (especially those of the clergy). Hircanus stands accused of tyranny, for subverting the causes of law and justice and replacing them with his own arbitrary will.[37] John uses the label "tyrant" in the *Entheticus Maior* in a looser and less rigorous manner than he will in his later writing; here it is hurled as an epithet rather than applied as an analytical category of political thought. The tyrant stands in for the bad monarch pure and simple, instead of denoting a ruler who commits a particular sort of evil.[38] In turn, John's political teaching appears to be little more than the empirical generalization that bad times are the result of a bad ruler. Hence the well-meaning but inexperienced courtier must do all he can to

---

[34] *Entheticus*, 1:154–61, 166–77.

[35] *Entheticus*, 1:178–81, 184–87.

[36] *Entheticus*, 1:188–89.

[37] *Entheticus*, 1:190–93.

[38] See Cary J. Nederman, "The Changing Image of the Tyrant: The Reign of King Stephen in John of Salisbury's Thought," *Nottingham Medieval Studies* 33 (1989): 1–20.

influence the new ruler to avoid pursuing the discredited policies of his predecessors. John may hardly be called optimistic about the possibility of Becket's
success in this regard. "I fear that the chancellor is striving in vain that the proud
court should change its customs," he says, inasmuch as corrupt "morals have
been introduced into the court by that rope-dancer [Henry II] who defends by
the law of his grandfather whatever he attempts."[39] John warns of the "little
snares" that await a courtier "who speaks the truth." He advises instead to "take
care that you do not perish by your garrulity," since those who state their minds
honestly are targeted for exile by "the false philosopher," that is, the tyrant.[40]
John is thus not above recommending a bit of pious deception in order to negotiate the duplicity of the court and to achieve one's goal: "That trick is good by
which one profits in a useful manner, when through it rejoicing, life, and salvation are procured."[41] The pragmatism of this message, which adopts the reasoning one would expect from a seasoned courtier, contrasts strikingly with the tone
of Parts I and II, which display the innocence of someone largely unfamiliar
with the conduct of public affairs.

John "instructs" his book to deliver the message about the dangers of court
directly to his intended reader, and then return immediately. But the road back
from court is equally precarious, littered with moral obstacles. Most of the remaining stanzas of Part III are devoted to depicting the dubious characters
whom one is likely to encounter while traveling.[42] The inns and hotels are populated by men who represent a cross-section of society's evils, no better than the
courtiers whose snares have just been escaped. Even once a return home to Canterbury has been accomplished, the threats to one's virtue do not end: the cloister, too, contains residents who strive after purely earthly goods rather than seeking to love and honor God through learning and reflection. Flattery, intrigue,
jealousy, slander, and boastfulness occur as commonly in the cloister as in the
world at large.[43] The impression John leaves is that no communal or institutional
setting can assure the prevention of human corruption.

Where, then, is a person with a sincere desire to live honorably to turn? The
answer to this question occupies John in the final section of the *Entheticus
Maior*, a brief coda of fewer than one hundred lines that meditates on the lessons
of the work. He repeats his counsel that keeping oneself in the company of true
philosophers—that is, men of good morals and deep faith—constitutes the key
to resisting vice. In order to reach an accurate judgment about whom to befriend,
in turn, one must seek the advice of the ancient writers and of wise teachers. The
lessons of these authorities form the necessary and indispensable guide to the
virtues. John's message is not one of despair. One may indeed live a worthy
existence on earth, whether as a courtier or as a churchman. Yet John certainly
believes that the path to achieving a good life is difficult and that responsibility

[39] *Entheticus*, 1:200–1.
[40] *Entheticus*, 1:202–3.
[41] *Entheticus*, 1:198–99.
[42] *Entheticus*, 1:204–11.
[43] *Entheticus*, 1:210–19.

falls squarely on the individual alone. At this stage in his intellectual development, he has no more concrete suggestions for reforming the political and ecclesiastical (or for that matter, educational) system of his day in order to improve
the conditions for virtue or at least to discourage the spread of vice. In the *Entheticus Maior*, John displays a clear awareness of the problems confronted by
the cleric in public life, but he has barely begun to consider potential solutions.
That element of his humanism—the recognition that it is both possible and de-
sirable to promote change in the world—appears only with his move from satirical poetry to philosophical prose.

Policraticus

In many ways, the *Policraticus* (subtitled *Of the Frivolities of Courtiers and the
Footprints of Philosophers*) extends and embellishes upon the intellectual enterprise commenced in the *Entheticus Maior*. Unlike his early verse, however, John
attempts in the *Policraticus* to identify and defend the salient principles of a
well-ordered and virtue-inducing political life. What the *Entheticus Maior*
lacked, in short, was sustained philosophical argument of the sort found in the
Policraticus. Thus, the *Policraticus* commonly receives acclaim as the first
complete work of political theory written during the Latin Middle Ages. But the
contents of its eight books (representing approximately 250,000 words) mark it
as far more than a theoretical treatise on politics. It equally contributes to the
fields of moral theology, speculative philosophy, legal procedure, and biblical
commentary, yet it always remains a deeply personal meditation as well. The
Policraticus is perhaps best described as the philosophical memoir of one of the
most learned courtier-bureaucrats of twelfth-century Europe. Although the
meaning of the title *Policraticus*—like "Entheticus" a pseudo-Greek neolo-
gism—has been debated, it seems to have been invented by John in order to
convey the implication of classical learning and erudition as well as to capture
the political content of the work.[44]

John constructs a bridge between his earlier writing and the current work by
introducing the latter with a prefatory verse, the *Entheticus in Policraticum* (or
Entheticus Minor). This 306-line poem is culled primarily from the text of Part 3
of the *Entheticus Maior* and also employs the technique of *prosopopeia* in order
to address its audience (presumably Thomas Becket, to whom the *Policraticus* is
explicitly dedicated). But the resemblances between the two poems should not
be overstated. The *Entheticus Minor* drops satire in favor of a more serious,
moralistic tone. The poem (that is, the reader) is lectured about avoidance of the
generally frivolous attitude that is found not only at court but also throughout
society, in the ecclesiastical as well as secular realms.[45] (It is not difficult to detect a connection between this point and the treatment of both lay and clerical

---

[44] Keats-Rohan, viii–ix.
[45] *Entheticus*, 1:238–39. There is also an edition of the *Entheticus Minor* in Keats-
Rohan, 9–19.

corruption in the later books of the *Policraticus*.) The poem must take care about how and with whom to speak. Among those who are not wholly trustworthy, it is best to dissimulate by feigning the language and dress of other cultures, lest the true purpose of the book's mission be uncovered.[46] There is a sense of foreboding and danger evident in the *Entheticus Minor* that is absent from the preceding work: public life is now a real threat for John, not mainly an object of humorous observations. The *Entheticus Minor* thus signals that the prose work that follows, while echoing themes addressed in the *Entheticus Maior*, will depart from it in important ways.

Although scholars have sometimes expressed doubt about the internal coherence of the *Policraticus*, a clear logical structure to its arguments (as well as a methodological cohesion and a consistent set of substantive principles) may be discerned. The first three books of the treatise reflect critically upon the socalled "frivolities" of courtiers, by which John means the range of activities and luxuries that promote private interest at the expense of public utility. Those who spend an excessive amount of time and energy indulging in frivolous pursuits not only harm themselves and violate their duties defined by natural law, but they detract from the common good.[47] In Books 4–6, John turns to a description of the right ordering of the political community, identifying the proper functions to be performed not merely by rulers, but also by each and every part of society. Finally, Books 7 and 8 survey the true and false teachings about human happiness that produce either wisdom and virtue, on the one hand, or corruption and vice, on the other. Before he closes the *Policraticus*, John discusses the problem of what can and should be done to solve the problems caused by the spread of "false" (essentially Epicurean) doctrines of happiness that seem to be widely held at court and beyond.

As the study of John's career makes plain, the final arrangement of the text of the *Policraticus* does not reflect the original order of its composition. In 1156 or 1157, during his period of self-proclaimed "disfavor" when he was exiled from Canterbury due to Henry II's anger, John began to write a prose work that attempted to demonstrate the foundations of the good life for man and to demystify the false images of happiness propounded by those of his contemporaries who (knowingly or unwittingly) advocated the hedonistic doctrines of Epicureanism. This treatise, which represented a sort of self-consolation in a time of political disrepute (evidently modeled on Boethius's *Consolation of Philosophy*), came to form the bulk of the chapters in Books 7 and 8 of the finished *Policraticus*.

After his recall to active service in Archbishop Theobald's household, John undertook to transform his self-consolatory meditation into a full-fledged treatise of advice to his fellow clerical bureaucrats about the potential misfortunes of life at secular and ecclesiastical courts, and why they must be avoided. In particular, such concerns apparently stimulated John to compose the more overtly political sections of the *Policraticus* (Books 4, 5, and 6) in which he articulates a theory of government and society which, if realized, would better preserve the

---

[46] *Entheticus*, 1:230–31, 236–39.
[47] Keats-Rohan, 28–29.

physical and spiritual safety of civil servants like himself as well as their princes and subjects. John thereby broadened his concern from the good life for the individual man to the good life for the entire political body. The completion of the *Policraticus* in its final form is dated, on both internal and external evidence, to the early autumn of 1159, although it is entirely possible that he continued to revise it lightly in later years.

Like most works of medieval philosophy, the *Policraticus* depends heavily upon authoritative sources as a means for extending and enhancing its arguments. Thinkers such as John believed that the case for a specific claim was strengthened not only by rational demonstration but also by the antiquity and the eminence of the authorities one could adduce in support of it. Consequently, we encounter throughout the *Policraticus* extensive quotations from and citations of both pagan and Christian sources. John's most important authority, both quantitatively and qualitatively, is Scripture. While his careful and often subtle use of biblical imagery and texts reveals a thorough knowledge of both Testaments, he manifests a clear preference throughout the *Policraticus* for the Old Testament, especially the books of the prophets and of wisdom. At times, the *Policraticus* even engages in biblical commentary. Much of Book 4, for instance, is taken up with exegesis of a passage from Deuteronomy, by means of which John demonstrates the salient features of the good ruler. John is also conversant with the Fathers of the Latin Church and other early Christian authors. The *Policraticus* displays a particular fondness for Augustine and Jerome, and for the historical writings of Orosius, but there are few available writers of the patristic age whom John fails to cite.

The *Policraticus* is perhaps best known, however, for the number and range of its references to the texts and doctrines of pagan antiquity. Indeed, the scope of John's learning once earned him the title of the best-read man of the twelfth century.[48] John's classical education was particularly thorough in the areas of rhetoric, philosophy, and poetry. He seems to have been familiar with all the available works of Cicero—although not, of course, Cicero's two major works of political theory, *De re publica* (except for Book 6, the "Dream of Scipio") and *De legibus*, the ideas contained in which he knew only through Christian intermediaries such as Augustine and Lactantius. John presents himself as a follower of Cicero in both language and method, perhaps recognizing a kindred spirit joined by similar predicaments as philosophers involved in political affairs.[49] In any case, the criticism of Cicero offered in the *Entheticus Maior* disappears in the *Policraticus*, which is written in a language calculated to imitate the style of the great Roman rhetorician. Perhaps even more significantly, John identifies himself throughout the *Policraticus* as a "devotee of Academic dispute. . . on

---

[48] Reginald Lane Poole, *Illustrations of the History of Medieval Thought and Learning* (London: SPCK, 1920), 191.

[49] Birger Munk-Olsen, "L'humanisme de Jean de Salisbury, un cicéronien au 12e siècle," in *Entretiens sur la Renaissance du 12e siècle*, ed. Maurice de Gandillac and Edouard Jeauneau (Paris: Mouton, 1968), 53–69.

the authority of Cicero."[50] This is an intellectual commitment that has profound repercussions for the substance of John's thought.

In addition to Cicero, John integrated into the *Policraticus* many citations from the major and minor Latin poets; among his favorites were Virgil, Horace, Juvenal, Lucan, and Ovid. Yet good reason exists to doubt whether the breadth of John's classical Latin quotations and allusions in the *Policraticus* was matched by thorough firsthand acquaintance with the texts to which he refers. It has been demonstrated, for instance, that his use of passages from the pagan authors Aulus Gellius, Suetonius, and Frontinus does not reflect direct exposure to their writings.[51] Rather, John relied on *florilegia* (or books of extracts) compiled by later editors that were readily available to him at the libraries of Canterbury. Hence John's classical learning was not as extensive as a cursory reading of the *Policraticus* might suggest.

Of the philosophical and literary works of the Greeks, John knew little in comparison with later centuries; like virtually all Westerners of his time, he read no Greek. He could acknowledge the bare existence of Homer, Herodotus, Pythagoras, and Socrates, and he was occasionally able to ascribe specific doctrines to them. He knew some of Plato's thought by means of an available Latin translation of and commentary on the *Timaeus*. Perhaps most importantly, John was closely attuned to the reintroduction of Aristotle's writings into the Latin West. He may have been one of the first in the Middle Ages to be familiar with the entirety of Aristotle's Organon (the six Aristotelian treatises on logic). Even though Aristotle's moral and political writings would not be circulated in Western Christendom until the thirteenth century, John was able to glean from the Organon many important Aristotelian ideas (such as the doctrine of the golden mean and the psychology of moral character) which he incorporated into the social philosophy of the *Policraticus*.[52]

Yet the general absence of classical models of politics created for John something of a dilemma, since his intellectual instincts resisted the postulation of innovative concepts unsupported by long-standing tradition. His solution is one that was not uncommon during the Middle Ages: he created a bogus authority—in essence, he perpetrated a forgery—in order to legitimize ideas that were otherwise original to him. The archetypical instance of this in the *Policraticus* is his reference to a work called the "Instruction of Trajan," purportedly a letter composed by the Roman imperial writer Plutarch. John attributes to this treatise many of the most significant and insightful features of his political theory, especially the claim that the political system can be analyzed in detail as an organism

---

[50] Keats-Rohan, 25–26. On John's Academic proclivities in the *Policraticus*, see Cary J. Nederman, *Worlds of Difference: European Discourses of Toleration, c.1100–c.1550* (University Park: Pennsylvania State University Press, 2000), 48–51.

[51] This conclusion stems from the diligent research of Janet Martin, summarized in "John of Salisbury as Classical Scholar," in *WJS*, 179–201.

[52] See the studies collected in Cary J. Nederman, *Medieval Aristotelianism and its Limits: Classical Traditions in Moral and Political Philosophy, 12th–15th Centuries*, Variorum Collected Studies 565 (London: Ashgate, 1997).

or living body whose parts are mutually devoted to and dependent upon one another. In fact, the framework for the whole of Books 5 and 6 is allegedly lifted from the "Instruction of Trajan." Yet there is no independent evidence for the existence of a work by Plutarch (or some later Plutarchian imitator) as described by John. And when authors subsequent to him cite the "Instruction of Trajan," it is always on the basis of the report of the *Policraticus*. Hence, scholars now usually conclude that the "Instruction of Trajan" was actually a convenient fiction fashioned by John as a cloak for that intellectual novelty commonly despised in his day.[53] Moreover, this gives us good reason to believe that when John refers to other unknown sources, he may be performing a similar sleight-of-hand before his audience.

To the modern reader, one of the most peculiar features of the *Policraticus* is John's regular and prolonged use of *exempla*, that is, stories told to illustrate or exemplify a lesson or doctrine. Many chapters of the text are little more than a collection of such tales strung together with no apparent organization or interconnection. The sources for these *exempla* vary widely; many are biblical, some derive from classical or patristic historians, and a few are even the products of John's own experiences at papal and royal courts. The complaint is sometimes heard that he is wholly unconcerned about the actual historical significance—let alone the accuracy—of the stories and events he recounts. John's reliance upon *exempla* does not meet standards set by modern historical scholarship. Yet the use of *exempla* must nevertheless be taken very seriously.[54] The *Policraticus* is as much a work of moral edification as of philosophical speculation. It is intended to have practical relevance and value by imparting to John's contemporaries a code of conduct applicable to the unsettled circumstances of the clerical administrator. Thus, John's examples are oriented to the demonstration of how abstract principles of moral and political behavior may be employed in everyday life. Like the parables of Jesus in the New Testament, the *exempla* of the *Policraticus* teach general lessons through concrete stories. Sometimes these lessons pertain to the translation of vicious or sinful beliefs into action, while at other times they illustrate the ways in which goodness and faith manifest themselves. But in all cases, John's *exempla* are meant to help the reader to bridge the gap between abstract moral discourse, on the one hand, and the actual conditions in which human beings find themselves, on the other.

There is a further dimension to the use of *exempla* in the *Policraticus* that runs to the heart of the methodology John employs. Peter von Moos has pointed out how John often deploys his *exempla* in apparently contradictory ways, forcing

---

[53] Hans Liebeschütz is the scholar most closely associated with this development; see his classic "John of Salisbury and Pseudo-Plutarch," *Journal of the Warburg and Courtauld Institutes* 6 (1943): 33–39. Max Kerner is perhaps the leading dissenter, his arguments for a pre-existing text given in "Randbemerkungen zur *Institutio Traiani*," in *WJS*, 203–6. Without rehearsing the debate, the position pioneered by Liebeschütz continues to be convincing.

[54] For what follows, see Peter von Moos, "The Use of *Exempla* in the *Policraticus* of John of Salisbury," in *WJS*, 207–61.

the reader to reason for himself about the truth that stands behind the ostensible conflict. This precisely adopts the intellectual method pioneered by Peter Abelard, John's revered teacher, in his *Sic et non*, which reproduced seemingly contrasting statements from Scripture and other orthodox sources and leaves it to the individual to reconcile them. John would appear, then, to have an epistemological agenda supporting his use of *exempla*—one derived from, or at least indebted to, Abelard.[55] The salient conclusion reached by John is that the theory of mind proposed by the moderate skepticism of the Ciceronian New Academy requires a measure of intellectual liberty and openness to debate and discussion.[56] An Abelardian approach to discovery is therefore necessary: "One is free to doubt and inquire up to the point when truth shines forth from the comparison of positions as though from the clash of ideas."[57] Von Moos suggests, in turn, that the composition of the *Metalogicon* was made necessary by John's need to lend support to this vital methodological premise of his work (a view that will be examined shortly). In this epistemological project, the underpinnings of John's humanism may be viewed: the truth, while available to human beings, is largely hidden and therefore requires effort and inspiration to be recovered. The *Policraticus* deploys *exempla* as a means of encouraging its audience to hone and refine reason in the quest for knowledge.

The guiding principles of method that render the *Policraticus* far more than a rambling and disjointed collection of stories and observations are matched by a number of unifying themes that lend intellectual coherence to the treatise and also point to its humanistic character. Perhaps the most noteworthy feature of the *Policraticus* in this connection is the relationship between secular and spiritual spheres and powers. John is not strictly a "hierocratic" thinker, if that term denotes the claim that all political authority flows from God through the Church to earthly rulers, so that the use of power is always to be regulated and limited by ecclesiastical officials.[58] Instead, he permits to secular powers a measure of genuine independence from interference by the Church in the conduct of temporal government. Like the soul in the body, he asserts, the priesthood fixes the general aims of political institutions (namely, the conditions necessary for salva-

---

[55] Peter von Moos, *Geschichte als Topik* (Hildesheim: Georg Olms Verlag, 1988), 238–309. On Abelard's method of reasoning, see Constant Mews, "Peter Abelard and the Enigma of Dialogue," in *Beyond the Persecuting Society: Religious Toleration Before the Enlightenment*, ed. John Christian Laursen and Cary J. Nederman (Philadelphia: University of Pennsylvania Press, 1998), 23–52.

[56] In conversation, Sabina Flanagan pointed out to me that both William of St. Thierry and St. Bernard employ the term "Academici" in connection with Abelard and his students. See Jean Leclercq, "Les lettres de Guillaume de St-Thierry à Saint Bernard," *Revue Benedictine* 79 (1969): 375–91, a reference for which I am indebted to Dr. Flanagan. Is it possible that John fully understood that his defense of the "Academic" method cloaked his intellectual sympathies with Abelard?

[57] Webb, 2:122.

[58] For what follows, see Cary J. Nederman and Catherine Campbell, "Kings, Priests, and Tyrants: Spiritual and Temporal Power in John of Salisbury's *Policraticus*," *Speculum* 66 (1991): 572–90.

tion).[59] But the ruler is responsible for ensuring and supervising the actual physical welfare of those whom he governs. Thus there exists a common good within the community unique and distinct from, although conducive to, the ultimate spiritual end of salvation. It is the promotion of this common good—the realization of a just society on earth—that forms the primary temporal duty of princes and of all their subjects.

John expresses the idea of earthly well-being by developing an extensive analogy between the living body and the political community. Claiming to adapt the main arguments of the forged "Instruction of Trajan," John compares the ruler to the head, the senate (counselors) to the heart, the judges and proconsuls to the senses, the hands and arms to tax collectors and soldiers, the household servants to the flanks, the fiscal officers to the stomach and intestines, and the peasants and artisans to the feet.[60] (The significance of the fact that the letter is purportedly written by Plutarch, an author who was little-known but well regarded in medieval Europe, to Trajan, the "most virtuous pagan," ought not to be lost on us.[61]) Although organic metaphors enjoyed a long tradition in Western social and political thought,[62] and John may have derived his version from his teacher Robert Pullen,[63] the image contained in the *Policraticus* stands out for several reasons. First, John develops the analogy to a far greater extent than does any preceding author: it frames the discussion of the well-ordered community and its parts that comprises the entirety of Books 5 and 6 of the *Policraticus*, amounting to nearly a quarter of its text. John fleshes out in detail all of the duties associated with the functions necessary for a healthy political body, while also explaining how the tasks assigned to each part stand in a necessary relation to the whole. Second, he stresses the reciprocal character of the well-ordered political community. Unlike most preceding thinkers, for whom organic images of public life were simply a way of emphasizing political hierarchy and subordination, John holds that all parts must consciously work together in order to achieve a common good that none of them can attain independently. In his version of the oft-told story of the revolt of the members of the body against the stomach, John stresses the cooperative dependence of each limb and organ upon the others.[64] Finally, John's deployment of the organic metaphor is inclusive. He embraces the participation of all social classes—including those associated with the "mechanical arts"—in the life of the community.[65] His main criterion for

---

[59] Webb, 1:282.

[60] Webb, 1:283.

[61] See Marcia L. Colish, "The Virtuous Pagan: Dante and the Christian Tradition," in *The Unbounded Community: Papers in Christian Ecumenism in Honor of Jaroslav Pelikan*, ed. William Caferro and Duncan G. Fisher (New York: Garland, 1996), 43–91.

[62] Tilman Struve, *Die Entwicklung der organologischen Staatsauffassung im Mittelalter* (Stuttgart: Anton Hiersemann, 1978), 10–122.

[63] See Liebeschütz, *Mediaeval Humanism in the Life and Writings of John of Salisbury*, 23–24.

[64] Webb, 2:71–72.

[65] Webb, 2:58–59.

political identity seems to be the contribution that a segment of the body makes to the functional good of the whole. Peasants and artisans contribute very materially to the social unit, and therefore deserve to be accorded a confirmed place in society. In sum, the *Policraticus* recognizes the increasing complexity and diversity of political life during the Middle Ages, which the bodily analogy is employed to capture.

John's doctrine of the different but interrelated aims within the community parallels his teachings about moral virtue and personal flourishing. As a Christian, he accepts that the ultimate goal of human existence is eternal life in the presence of God. But for him this does not diminish the importance of achieving goodness and happiness on earth. Rather, the *Policraticus* declares that men are morally bound to seek their own temporal fulfillment through the acquisition of knowledge and the practice of virtue. Such a way of life, while it can never earn the gift of God's grace from which arises salvation, only confirms the completeness and joyfulness that are the special attributes of the faithful Christian.[66] John consequently attempts to fuse classical and Christian values and to demonstrate a fundamental consistency between ancient moral philosophy and medieval moral theology.

John believes that, at least so far as life on earth is concerned, men play an active role in creating their own happiness both as individuals and as political creatures. He claims that the political system must be guided by the principles of nature, which he regards in Stoic fashion as "the best guide to living."[67] Yet nature does not strictly determine human behavior. Rather, men must actively cooperate with nature by means of experience and practice. Human beings conform themselves to the course suggested by nature, a feat that is accomplished by extending their knowledge and realizing their virtue. This is true at the personal as well as the social level. Just as people cultivate their own individual qualities by improving upon their natural attributes through effort and education, so they achieve a well-ordered political community by acknowledging and performing the natural duties demanded by justice toward their fellow creatures. Nature may fix the path of the good life, but men must exercise their minds and wills so as to discover and follow this route.

It is obvious, then, that John's political and moral philosophies are inextricably interwoven. Nowhere is this more evident than in his notion of moderation. John contends in Aristotelian fashion that the golden mean is a structural feature of all the virtues which individual persons may acquire; justice, courage, and the like are middle points between dual vices of excess and deficiency. For this reason, John insists throughout the *Policraticus* that while many sorts of conduct (such as hunting, banqueting, drinking, gaming, and so on) are vicious if performed often or regularly, they may be condoned if done in moderation for the purpose of recreation.[68] "If moderation is displayed," John remarks, "I do not

---

[66] Keats-Rohan, 175.

[67] For example, see Keats-Rohan, 185, 232; Webb, 2:59–60.

[68] On this theme, see Cary J. Nederman and John Brückmann, "Aristotelianism in John of Salisbury's *Policraticus*," *Journal of the History of Philosophy* 21 (1983): 210–16.

judge it disgraceful for a wise man to dwell occasionally on these pleasures of the senses; as is oftentimes said, nothing is proper without the mean. It is appropriate for even the wise man to enjoy leisure occasionally ... in order that he may be to some extent reinvigorated and revived."[69] In sum, moderation is the touchstone of a morally correct (and ultimately, happy) life. Only very rarely does John insist that an activity associated with courtly frivolity is entirely wrong or forbidden. One example of this is his condemnation of occult and astrological practices that seem to have enjoyed popularity during his time. To attempt to foresee the future, he reasons, is to claim for oneself the sort of knowledge that God alone enjoys. Our minds are capable of knowing only in a contingent and fallible way that prevents us from attaining certain truth about future events on earth.[70] His unusually strenuous rejection of all divination and related practices stems from their roots in human pride and arrogance. They are incompatible with the limits of human intellect and thus admit of no golden mean.

Moderation simultaneously constitutes the salient characteristic of the good ruler in the *Policraticus*. John's king exercises power in a moderate fashion, neither releasing his subjects wholly to the caprice of their own volition nor controlling their behavior so strenuously that they become incapable of using their legitimate free will. Royal moderation is equivalent to respect for the proper sphere of liberty that belongs to each and every member of the political community. John stresses that even a zealous insistence upon the virtue of subjects is a violation of the terms of moderate government. The king properly accords his people a sufficient measure of personal liberty that they may commit errors, at least so long as their sins endanger neither the safety of orthodox faith nor the security of the temporal polity.[71] The ability of an individual to acquire virtue requires the training and exercise of the will, which means that one will make mistakes on occasion. Moreover, the best way for people to correct their faults is when their fellows enjoy the freedom to speak their minds and to point out moral or intellectual error. John was fond of pointing out how even the Romans permitted their slaves the "December liberty" of openly criticizing their masters.[72] Readers of the *Policraticus* who encounter the elevation of the king to the status of "the minister of God" and the servant of divine law may be tempted to ascribe to John a doctrine of the "divine right of kings."[73] But John is careful not to exalt the king too greatly: the good ruler must still restrain himself with the bridle of law and hold back his will, and he must maintain humility in his relations with his subjects.[74] The king is defined by moderation in all his deeds and decrees.

Why, given his position of unchallenged power, will a good ruler continue to keep himself in check? His own ingrained moral character, the result of a

[69] Webb, 2:315.
[70] Keats-Rohan, 121–22.
[71] Keats-Rohan, 263.
[72] Webb, 2:217–25.
[73] Keats-Rohan, 233.
[74] Keats-Rohan, 254–58.

careful program of moral instruction, necessarily guides him to seek justice and respect divine dictates. The king is conceived by John to be the characteristically good man raised to royal office. It bears emphasis that John's conception of the nature of political power is an entirely personalized one: the incumbent makes the office. The king's disposition to follow the path of moderation is reinforced, moreover, by the rewards that he receives: honored among men, he guarantees his own peaceful reign and a safe succession for his heirs; beloved of God, he will receive the gift of salvation in the afterlife. "Kings can flourish and abound with the most sweet worldly things," John proclaims, "and yet can pick the most useful fruits of eternity." Nor does he suppose that such deserts pertain only to the most righteous of rulers. Rather, "to refuse evil is a great thing in them [princes], even if they do no great goodness, provided that they do not destroy their subjects by indulging in evil."[75] The king who refrains from misusing his great powers and who pursues policies that maintain the harmonious order of the community assures happiness (on earth and in heaven) for himself, his progeny, and his subjects.

By contrast, immoderate conduct (that which exceeds the mean) is regarded by John to be the defining mark of tyranny. The discussion of tyranny is one of the best known and most influential features of the *Policraticus*. Preceding classical and medieval authors construed tyranny in terms of the evil or destructive use of public authority, a view John himself adopts in the *Entheticus Maior*. By contrast, the *Policraticus* identifies the tyrant as any person who joins the ambitious desire to curtail the liberty of others with the power to accomplish this goal.[76] As a result, John's theory of tyranny is generic in the sense that it permits a tyrant to emerge in any walk of life. Specifically, he catalogues three classes of tyrants: the private tyrant, the public tyrant, and the ecclesiastical tyrant. Private tyranny occurs when any private person employs the authority allotted to him so as to dominate or limit the legitimate freedom of someone else. The private variety of tyrant may appear in the household, the manor, the shire, or anywhere that power is wielded. The suppression of private tyranny John assigns to royal government, since the king is charged with primary responsibility for the enforcement of law and the protection of all sections of the community.[77]

The second category of tyranny—the ecclesiastical tyrant—is perhaps the most surprising one to the modern reader. John devotes nearly as much attention in the *Policraticus* to the criticism of the behavior of clerics and priests as of temporal officials.[78] In particular, he realizes that there is great scope for churchmen to abuse their powers and hence to become ecclesiastical tyrants whose ambition for the offices and wealth of the church requires them to disregard the spiritual nourishment of the body of Christian believers. He is less forthcoming, however, about the appropriate method for the punishment of ecclesiastical tyrants. In general, he prefers to leave such correction to the deter-

---

[75] Keats-Rohan, 265.
[76] Webb, 2:160–62.
[77] Webb, 2:364.
[78] Webb, 2:162–201.

mination of the Roman pontiff, although he does acknowledge that once a cleric or priest has been stripped of ecclesiastical immunity he may be prosecuted for his crimes by earthly authorities.[79] But of greater significance, John's analysis draws theoretical force from its refusal to excuse any sphere in which power is exercised from the possibility of tyrannical conduct.

Finally, when supreme monarchic authority passes into the hands of an ambitious man the form of tyranny becomes specifically public, insofar as the office of the prince differs from other forms of power in secular society. The prince, as the pinnacle of temporal political organization, represents both the ordinary assurance of the security and liberty of his subjects and the authoritative source of earthly law and jurisdiction within his realm. Thus, a public tyrant is inevitably accompanied by the destruction of the other parts of the community as well. In order to combat the threat of a public tyrant, John believes that the remaining members of the polity are charged with a duty—stemming from the principle of justice itself—to criticize, to correct, and (if necessary) even to kill a tyrannical ruler. Moreover, he takes this duty to be a generalized one: it pertains not merely to royal magistrates but to all segments of the body politic. Everyone is equally obligated (by their membership in society) to enforce the terms of justice, since John understands the duty of justice in Ciceronian terms as demanding that one not merely refrain from the commission of injury but also ensure that harm is not done to one's fellow human beings.[80] Because tyranny is extremely harmful to the whole community, the just person is bound to oppose it.

John's controversial claim that it may be morally prescribed to slay a particularly egregious tyrant requires special attention. Some scholars have tried to argue that John never meant to justify the murder of bad rulers in either theory or practice, but only to warn rulers that "God ultimately assures that all tyrants meet a bad end."[81] To deny practical implications or theoretical foundations of John's statements about the death of tyrants in Book 8 neglects an important dimension of the *Policraticus*, however. Central to his approach to philosophy was the belief that people have duties both to their fellow citizens and to God to act for the common good. With no idea of an institutional method for limiting the power of monarchs (such as deposition or impeachment), John very reasonably turns to personal remedies when confronted with an evil ruler whose continued governance threatens the moral and spiritual health of the community. And when persuasion fails to be effective, violence may be necessary and even laudable.[82] John is careful in *Policraticus* to stipulate that no one should rush to kill a tyrant: correction, patience, and prayer must precede action. Moreover, John closely regulates the way in which a tyrant may legitimately be eliminated. "Not that I do not believe that tyrants are to be removed from the community, but they

---

[79] Webb, 2:364.

[80] Keats-Rohan, 272–73.

[81] See Jan van Laarhoven, "Thou Shalt NOT Slay a Tyrant! The So-called Theory of John of Salisbury," in *WJS*, 319–41.

[82] Keats-Rohan, 230.

are to be removed without loss of religion and honor."[83] The suggestion that there is an appropriate time and method for slaying a tyrant indicates directly John's belief in the existence of a moral duty to perform such an act. God remains, of course, the final judge of anyone who lifts a hand against a tyrant: only the person whose intent is pure and genuine will be absolved by Him. Divine retribution constitutes an adequate check, in John's view, on abuse of his teaching about tyrannicide.

The key themes of the *Policraticus* in many ways reflect the concerns of twelfth-century political, intellectual, and ecclesiastical life. Indeed, John's very conception of philosophy compels us to examine his thought in relation to its historical points of reference. Throughout his writings, he stresses that philosophical inquiry ought not to be a specialized, dry, and obscure pursuit, but rather an integral feature of an active and dutiful life within the political arena, a life devoted to the service of God and His children. In proposing the political ideas of the *Policraticus*, he sought above all to illustrate the principle that philosophy is an aid to achieving the good life of both the individual and the whole community. The vitality of John's political thought consists primarily in its confrontation with the practical demands of politics in relation to the requirements of living well in an ethical and religious sense.

At the same time, John's work succeeds in making the philosophical analysis of politics intellectually respectable to his audience. The *Policraticus* aims to demonstrate that public affairs are not necessarily corrupt, but can instead be conducted in a philosophically satisfactory manner according to which human goodness and happiness are promoted and enhanced. Such a claim represents an important step toward the incorporation of political thought into the domain of speculative inquiry, from which medieval writers had largely excluded it up to John's own day. John richly deserves a reputation for having restored the theoretical study of public life to a place of prominence in the intellectual system of the West.

Metalogicon

If the reasons for John of Salisbury's composition of the *Policraticus* are relatively obvious and easy to trace, the motives behind his writing of the *Metalogicon* have remained more obscure. Short of the entirely unsubstantiated supposition of a surge of anti-educational fervor during the later 1150s, there seems nothing in the political and cultural environment of England (or even the continent) to spur his efforts. That the *Metalogicon* has certain affinities with the *Policraticus* is undeniable. The former adopts many of the same thematic elements as the latter. But attempts to treat the two works as parts of a larger whole, perhaps in the manner of a philosophical encyclopedia envisaged but unrealized by John, deny the intellectual integrity apparent in each treatise. Rather, the *Metalogicon*, like the *Policraticus*, shares its conceptual roots with the broad contours

---

[83] Webb, 2:378.

of the early satire in the *Entheticus Maior*; but also in common with the *Policraticus*, the *Metalogicon* demonstrates a philosophical depth and rigor absent in the preceding poem. Both the *Entheticus Maior* and the *Metalogicon* evince concern about the pedagogical assumptions that too often produce insubstantial and ineffective learning in the schools. Yet where John's poem merely mocks a certain breed of teachers and reprimands them for failing to capture the wisdom of their betters, his prose work both defends the general educational program of the schools against vehement criticism and delves into the principles appropriate to developing a worthwhile curriculum.

The *Metalogicon*, containing four books and running to somewhere over 50,000 words, is a much shorter and ostensibly more focused work than the *Policraticus*. The central theme holding the *Metalogicon* together is the defense of the study of the *trivium*, especially dialectic or logic. Book 1 addresses the critics of the scholastic curriculum (whom he labels "Cornificians," after Cornificius, the ancient Roman critic of Virgil); this book also lays out the basic precepts of grammar. The second, third, and fourth books survey logic both from a technical point of view (hence incorporating substantial commentary on Aristotle's Organon) and from a general perspective (why dialectical reasoning is necessary in order to ascertain truth and combat falsehood). Although the parts of the *Metalogicon* that contain comment on the basic works of classical logic may have been drafted by John as early as his school days in Paris, as was suggested in the preceding discussion of John's career, the *Metalogicon* was probably for the most part written during 1158 and 1159, that is, during the later stages of or immediately after the composition of the *Policraticus*. John's primary point is that the curriculum adopted by the schools, when taught in a balanced and reasonable manner, affords the best path toward wisdom, virtue, and the knowledge necessary for happiness and salvation. While John is not unmindful of the excesses that he encountered (both as student and as later observer) in Paris, he contends that these are the result of misapplied or misunderstood principles, not an inherent product of a scholastic education. John thus should be classified neither among the unreserved critics of the schools nor as an uncritical advocate of them. The *Metalogicon* is the work of a sympathetic reformer, who is accepting of the general outlines of scholastic learning, while still critical of some of the more extreme or invidious conceptions of advanced education on display in his time.

John's source materials for the *Metalogicon* are as rich and diverse as those that he employs in the *Policraticus*, albeit that the former is spiced with a more overtly Aristotelian flavor occasioned by the contents of Book 3 and much of Book 4. Aristotle is recurrently crowned with the title "The Philosopher" which was to become common in later scholastic circles.[84] Citations of Greek and Latin classics of literature and philosophy are woven into the text, as are references to the Fathers. Beyond Aristotle and, of course, Holy Scripture, John's favorite sources are Augustine, Boethius, Cicero, Isidore, Martianus Capella, and Quintilian. Where a

---

[84] John of Salisbury, *Metalogicon*, ed. J. B. Hall and K. S. B. Keats-Rohan (Turnhout: Brepols, 1991), 79–80, 145–46.

divergence of sources between the *Metalogicon* and the *Policraticus* occurs, it is conditioned largely by the differing purposes of the two works. Thus the ancient historians so prominently deployed in the *Policraticus* are nearly absent from the *Metalogicon*, but John alludes in the latter more directly to writings composed during his own times, including those by Peter Abelard, Gilbert of Poitiers, and Hugh of St. Victor, as well as to the classroom lessons of Bernard of Chartres, which he would have known by reputation only.

The *Metalogicon* contains perhaps John's most eloquent explanation of the proper attitude that one ought to adopt toward authorities—whether ancient or modern. On the one hand, he says, "Our own generation enjoys the legacy bequeathed by that which preceded it. We frequently know more . . . because we are supported by the strength of others and possess riches that we have inherited from our ancestors."[85] Authorities make readily available the wisdom of the ages. On the other hand, John disclaims "those who spurn the good things of their own day, and begrudge recommending their contemporaries to posterity." The ancients, too, made many mistakes, and their accomplishments must not be taken as authoritative in comparison with present learning.[86] John's own perspective is, rather, the balanced one that we might well expect of him. Adopting a metaphor that he ascribes to Bernard of Chartres, John compares the philosophers of his time to "dwarfs set upon the shoulders of giants. . . . We see more and farther than our predecessors not because we have a keener vision or great height, but because we are lifted up and borne aloft on their gigantic stature."[87] He supports this opinion by demonstrating how the study of logic builds from basic elements inherited from Aristotle into a substantial edifice of learning. John's account defends the conception of authority that evidently guided him in the *Policraticus* no less than in the *Metalogicon*.

Another feature common to the *Metalogicon* and the *Policraticus* is John's avowed methodological commitment to the moderate skepticism of the New Academy. In the Prologue of the *Metalogicon*, he announces, "Being an Academic in matters that are doubtful to a wise person, I cannot swear to the truth of what I say. Whether such propositions may be true or false, I am satisfied with probable certainty."[88] John distances his own skepticism from more radical views that deny the possibility of knowing truth (or very many truths) at all.[89] Yet he admits that, even if truth is susceptible to human comprehension, the process of achieving knowledge is burdensome. Echoing a remark made by Cicero in the *Academica*, John observes, "It is difficult to apprehend the truth, which (as our Academics say) is as obscure as if it lay at the bottom of a well."[90] Although he demonstrates some sympathy with St. Augustine's criticisms in *Contra Academicos* of Ciceronian skepticism, John returns often in the *Meta-*

---

[85] *Metalogicon*, 116.

[86] *Metalogicon*, 102.

[87] *Metalogicon*, 116.

[88] *Metalogicon*, 11; for similar statements, see 91, 145.

[89] *Metalogicon*, 168.

[90] *Metalogicon*, 76.

logicon to Cicero's methodological injunction against embracing insufficiently substantiated propositions too hastily in the quest for knowledge. To rush to judgment always inevitably leads to advocacy of doctrinaire and dogmatic positions.

In this way, the *Metalogicon* may be viewed as lending philosophical support to the principle of "logical probability" that stands behind the project of the *Policraticus*, in which John declares that "the judgments, whether motivated by love or hate, will one way or another go wrong . . . It is left to the free will of the reader to choose what path is to be followed, so that vice and infamous deceit have been performed at a distance from my name."[91] John's reader, in other words, will have to make up his own mind for himself. But how is the reader to do this so as to avoid "vice and deceit"? The *Metalogicon* provides precisely the key to logical analysis by means of which the understanding and discernment of the truth are most likely to be achieved. As von Moos has emphasized, the *Metalogicon* is thus a necessary complement to the *Policraticus*. The former work lays out the conceptual apparatus (derived not only from Cicero, but quite possibly also from Abelard and perhaps from Gilbert)[92] necessary for the appreciation of the philosophical integrity of the latter volume. Indeed, as K. S. B. Keats-Rohan has remarked, "It was also in *Metalogicon* that John worked out the theory of *logica probabilis* which Moos has shown to be the basis behind *Policraticus*. *Metalogicon* therefore provides the key to the understanding of *Policraticus* and is in some way ancillary to it."[93] Such an internal connection between the two books offers a significant part of the explanation of why John felt compelled to write the *Metalogicon* simultaneously with or close on the heels of the *Policraticus*. He felt that the lessons of the latter could not be adequately grasped without familiarity with the methodological precepts set out in the former.

Yet one may surmise that the vindication of probabilism attempted in the *Metalogicon* at the same time served another of John's intellectual concerns, this one of longer standing: the virulent attacks on the schools that he had observed during his years as a student in Paris (and perhaps also in more recent times). While this constitutes a less pressing reason for writing than the need to shore up the *Policraticus*, it may be that John had envisaged for some time a volume that commented upon and corrected the distorted ideas about a scholastic education that he had heard. Certainly, the enterprise of responding to critics of the curriculum dovetails very neatly with the defense of *logica probabilis* that makes up the main body of the *Metalogicon*.

Who were these critics and what were their complaints? As has been mentioned, John artfully veils the opponents whom he engages in the *Metalogicon* by calling them the followers of the pseudonymous "Cornificius." John never expressly identifies this "Cornificius," a fact that has led modern commentators

---

[91] Webb, 2:227.

[92] Von Moos, *Geschichte als Topik*, 239–40, 266–85, 366–67, 380–81. On the connection with Gilbert, see Clare Monagle, "Bookish Heresy: The Trial of Gilbert of Poitiers and Its Narratives" (M.A. Thesis, Department of History, Monash University, 1999), 99–127.

[93] Keats-Rohan, xii.

to argue about whether he was a composite of certain anti-intellectual tendencies rampant in the twelfth century.[94] John is quite simply confusing and contradictory about the question of Cornificius's identity. On the one hand, he invites the reader to associate Cornificius with an actual figure of the age with whom John had contact. He implies that Cornificius is someone who has directly opposed and goaded him with taunts and threats.[95] John accuses Cornificius of all manner of heinous acts, emphasizing the extreme obscenity and immorality of his personal code of conduct. He avers that he declines to attach an actual name to Cornificius only out of Christian charity and a desire not to reduce his refutation to a purely *ad hominem* attack (a claim that he surely intends ironically, since he proceeds to impugn quite pointedly his opponent's character).[96] Against the assertion that John is responding to a flesh-and-blood enemy stands a wealth of conflicting statements in the *Metalogicon*. John includes inconsistent remarks about, for example, the profession in which Cornificius is engaged (at various times, he appears as schoolmaster, courtier, monk, and businessman), the source of his dissatisfaction with the scholastic curriculum (it is too difficult, it cannot be learned, it is not profitable), and even his age. We are left, then, in a considerable quandary. Is John incorporating contradictory identifications in order to confuse his readers about the real target of his wrath? Or is he falsely implying the existence of a pseudonymous Cornificius in order to give a sense of immediacy to his riposte?

Perhaps the truth should be sought somewhere in between. John says that the Cornifician opponents of learning have taken up residence in a variety of locales, including the cloister, the medical practice, the classroom, the marketplace, and the court. Cornificius, we might say, has several faces, all of which are actual and concrete to John.[97] Cornificius thus is a many-headed beast or a shape-shifter, a protean man, who adopts a range of guises, yet always begins from the same erroneous and dangerous assumptions about education. Is it possible to detect any of the archetypes for Cornificius from our knowledge of John's biography? John was unafraid of engaging in intellectual and political combat with influential courtiers, perhaps the most notable of whom was Bishop Arnulf of Lisieux. Arnulf, who had engineered the disfavor of Henry II with John during 1156–1157, and thus had indirectly occasioned the composition of the *Policraticus*, is described in the later *Historia Pontificalis* as a courtier *par excellence*. According to John, Arnulf dabbled in "the frivolities of courtiers," he possessed a "smooth tongue," he lacked "fear of God," and maybe most importantly, he falsely claimed for himself the status of papal legate in order to

---

[94] See, most recently, Enrico Tacella, "Giovanni di Salisbury e i Cornificiani," *Sandalion* 3 (1980): 273–313; Rosemary B. Tobin, "The Cornifician Motif in John of Salisbury's *Metalogicon*," *History of Education* 13 (1984): 1–6; and Stephen C. Ferruolo, *The Origins of the University: The Schools of Paris and their Critics, 1100–1215* (Stanford: Stanford University Press, 1985), 141–43.

[95] *Metalogicon*, 10.

[96] *Metalogicon*, 14–15.

[97] *Metalogicon*, 20.

acquire private wealth. Furthermore, Arnulf's political ambition stands accused by John of ruining the Second Crusade.[98] The unmistakable loathing that John felt toward Arnulf (and that was evidently reciprocated) suggests that Henry's court may not have been the first time their paths had crossed. If the surmise of Frank Barlow is correct, they would have been students together in Paris during the later 1130s; perhaps some event of school days generated enmity between them.[99] Regardless of such speculation, John would certainly have known of Arnulf's educational background. Given their long-standing antipathy, it is not too difficult to imagine him as the model for the courtly Cornificius whose taunts supposedly provoked the composition of the *Metalogicon*.[100]

What may we surmise about the monastic aspect of Cornificius described in the *Metalogicon*? John observes, "In order that his sect may have greater license to slander others, the father of the family externally professes the religious life," cultivating friendships among the major monastic orders.[101] The information that John presents about Cornificius's views concerning education contains certain suggestive hints of Bernard of Clairvaux. Bernard had been one of the most outspoken and vehement critics of the Parisian schools, preaching and writing about the moral evils as well as heterodoxy to be found there.[102] John had an ambiguous relationship with Bernard. As we saw in surveying John's biography, Bernard's letter to Archbishop Theobald was responsible, at least in part, for the beginning of his career at Canterbury. Yet Bernard and his circle had also been responsible for the ecclesiastical persecution of two of John's most revered masters, Peter Abelard and Gilbert of Poitiers. John was prepared to treat Bernard as the "villain of the piece" in his later discussion of the events surrounding Gilbert's trial at Rheims in 1148 contained in the *Historia Pontificalis*.[103] One dimension of Cornificius's character that is especially reminiscent of Bernard is his adamant refusal to engage in direct disputation and rational debate with his adversaries.[104] Given Bernard's sterling reputation in the years immediately following his death (1153), however, John could hardly name him as an oppressive figure who opposed good doctrine. Still, Bernard's preaching against the schools in favor of monastic learning, his aversion to formal philosophical training, and his unwillingness to debate with those whose teachings he sought to suppress were all characteristics that John attributes to Cornificius. Bernard's actions,

---

[98] John of Salisbury, *Historia Pontificalis*, ed. Marjorie Chibnall (Oxford: Oxford University Press, 1986), 54–56.

[99] Frank Barlow, ed., *The Letters of Arnulf of Lisieux* (London: Royal Historical Society, 1939), xvii–xix.

[100] *Metalogicon*, 10, 19.

[101] *Metalogicon*, 22.

[102] On Bernard's criticism of the schools, see Ferruolo, *The Origins of the University*, 47–66, and Martha G. Newman, *The Boundaries of Charity: Cistercian Culture and Ecclesiastical Reform, 1098–1180* (Stanford: Stanford University Press, 1996), 37–41, 219–26.

[103] Monagle, "Bookish Heresy," 80.

[104] *Metalogicon*, 15.

albeit perhaps at the behest of William of St.-Thierry and others both within the Cistercian movement and without, effected a chill upon the climate of the schools just as the *Metalogicon* describes. Of course, the attribution of one face of Cornificius to Bernard is at best speculative, but it suggests a reason why John might wish to be cautious in publicly naming his opponents. In any case, more intensive study of the individuals with whom John had contact in the court, the cloister, the school, and the marketplace would probably yield the identities of various of his targets who are grouped together under the persona of Cornificius.

In spite of John's reluctance to unmask Cornificius, he has no qualms about specifying the reason he finds the Cornifician philosophy so repugnant. The Cornificians are primarily reviled as critics of rhetoric—a fact that some scholars have tended to overlook.[105] Only at the very close of his survey of Cornificius's ideas in Book 1 does John switch—somewhat abruptly—from the attack on rhetoric to the attack on logic.[106] This represents a strategic shift, according to John. Since they cannot possibly mute all human beings, the Cornificians attack an art allied with that of eloquent speech, namely, dialectic. But their true target, John proposes, remains rhetoric. They reject the value of rhetorical studies on the grounds that "eloquence ... is a gift that is either conceded or denied to each individual by nature."[107] For those to whom nature has granted facility with speech, practice is redundant and wasteful; those lacking original endowment can hardly expect to alter through education what nature has denied them, according to Cornificius.[108] John condemns this aspect of Cornifician teaching as particularly pernicious and invidious.

In the first place, to say that people cannot improve their linguistic abilities regardless of effort or training is empirically absurd. It is true, as any careful observer realizes, that human beings "learn how to talk in their nurses' arms before they receive instruction from doctors who occupy official chairs. The way one talks in manhood often smacks of the manner of speech of one's nurse. Sometimes the strenuous efforts of teachers cannot extricate one from habits imbibed at a tender age."[109] But this proves only that one must pay special attention to early education, not (as the Cornificians think) that nature is insusceptible to alteration or improvement. After all, John points out, "natural ability easily deteriorates when neglected" and "is strengthened by cultivation and care . . . Nothing is so strong and robust that it cannot be enfeebled by neglect, nothing so well constructed that it cannot be razed. On the other hand, diligent application can build up and preserve the lowest degree of natural talent."[110] In opposition to the Cornificians, then, the *Metalogicon* maintains that nature must be

---

[105] For example, Liebeschütz, *Mediaeval Humanism in the Life and Writings of John of Salisbury*, 85; more recently, Catherine Brown, *Contrary Things: Exegesis, Dialectic, and the Poetics of Didacticism* (Stanford: Stanford University Press, 1998), 44–45.

[106] *Metalogicon*, 27–28.

[107] *Metalogicon*, 22.

[108] *Metalogicon*, 25–26.

[109] *Metalogicon*, 23–24.

[110] *Metalogicon*, 27.

supplemented first by instruction and then by regular practice if eloquence is to flourish and prosper. Consequently, the blessings of eloquence accrue properly and fully to those who studiously devote themselves to internalizing and applying the rules of rhetoric. The Cornifician appeal to nature as the sole determinant of the eloquent man is bogus and deceptive, entailing a theologically unwarranted and empirically unsubstantiated presumption that "first nature" is perfect and complete in itself.[111]

In contrast to such erroneous opinions about the static quality of the human condition, John affirms the progress of mankind's rhetorical capacities through the appropriate combination of nature, grace, instruction, and application. In order to construct this argument, the *Metalogicon* draws upon elements of both Ciceronian and Aristotelian teachings. From Cicero's writings, John adapts a depiction of human society and civilization that depends on a combination of eloquent speech and reason (helped, of course, by an infusion of divine aid). He argues that social interaction constitutes an important wellspring of true (albeit partial, because mortal) human happiness (*beatitudo*). The *Metalogicon* regards nature as imprinted with a divine plan, "the most loving parent and best disposer of all that is." Thus, if nature has granted to humanity alone of all creatures the powers of speech and reason, this is so we may "obtain true happiness."[112] Adapting the model of the intercommunication of members that he also deployed in the *Policraticus*'s description of the body politic, John identifies social interaction as essential to the natural course that ought to guide human behavior. "One cannot imagine how any kind of happiness could exist entirely apart from mutual association and divorced from human society," John declares.[113] Therefore, whoever wishes to achieve supreme happiness is well advised to seek also earthly happiness in accordance with nature, that is, in association with fellow human beings, whose congregation constitutes "the sole and unique fraternity among the children of nature."[114] To imperil society by assailing the human capacity to improve rational powers—the key accusation that John levels against Cornificius—is to cut the human race off from the happiness that God has accorded in the present life, as well as to exclude the possibility of realizing the grace bestowed by Him.

Human sociability, in turn, depends upon the confluence of reason with speech, a case that John elaborates in typically Ciceronian fashion. Reason is insufficient for society, he observes, because it is an individualistic and internal faculty. Rather, reason must be made manifest by speech (and eloquent speech at that) if implicit human sociability is to be awakened and invigorated. Enlightened eloquence "has given birth to so many outstanding cities, has made friends and allies of so many kingdoms, and has united and bonded through love so many people."[115] Speech is the mechanism by which mute wisdom translates its

---

[111] *Metalogicon*, 25–26.
[112] *Metalogicon*, 12.
[113] *Metalogicon*, 12.
[114] *Metalogicon*, 12.
[115] *Metalogicon*, 13.

insights into public proclamations and persuades human beings to follow their natural inclinations to live together harmoniously. Should they be deprived of their faculty of language, even if they retained reason, they "would degenerate to the condition of brute animals, and cities would seem like corrals for livestock, rather than communities composed of human beings united by a common bond in order to live socially, serve one another, and cooperate as friends."[116] Speech renders such communal existence possible by convincing people to prefer the common good to private welfare. Hence the *Metalogicon* presumes that the bond of association, while in accordance with nature, results only from the active engagement and cooperation of human beings by improving their linguistic skills. All social arrangements and political institutions depend upon the civilizing effects of eloquent discourse in order to create and maintain human harmony.

Consequently, John proclaims that the Cornifician position, which denies that education can enhance natural human faculties, opposes "all cities and political life."[117] The Cornificians err by interpreting the natural weaknesses of humanity as permanent and irremediable, whereas the very fact that society exists disproves their case. Human nature (at least in its fallen state) is incapable of impelling association apart from the diligent application of reasoned speech. Community signifies the civilizing tendencies implicit within mankind that require extraction and refinement through education in order for nature's plan to be realized. The *Metalogicon* maintains that nature's endowment is only the point of departure. Human beings must develop their own capacities if they are to live in full accord with their natural inclinations.

The deployment of Cicero's account of human society in the *Metalogicon* in order to refute Cornificius is supplemented and reinforced by the use of Aristotelian epistemological, moral, and psychological concepts. John's opposition to Cornifician hyper-naturalism shares with Aristotle the general view that nature's role in human intellect is limited to the endowment of a capacity of the soul to acquire knowledge (*scientia*).[118] As a consequence, John teaches that the eloquent man becomes so by means of regular practice until he has firmly and forever internalized the principles of rhetoric. The essence of John's Aristotelian outlook is that the capacities ceded to man by "first nature" need to be completed by the formation of a second, acquired nature. Specifically, John teaches that what we know depends upon what we do: "Assiduous application . . . smoothes the way for understanding."[119] The ignorant man has been accustomed to false or incorrect precepts because his actions were not of a proper kind. Likewise, the knowledgeable individual has repeatedly practiced the behavior that accords with true knowledge of a discipline or skill. "Art, which becomes firmly established by use and practice, yields a faculty of accomplishing those things that are proper to it."[120] The argument is particularly compelling in the

---

[116] *Metalogicon*, 13–14.

[117] *Metalogicon*, 14.

[118] *Metalogicon*, 29–30.

[119] *Metalogicon*, 50.

[120] *Metalogicon*, 147.

case of eloquence. To propound abstract and obscure rules without concern for application provides no true instruction at all. "Rules alone are useless," the *Metalogicon* proclaims, since whoever learns the theoretical principles associated with rhetoric is by no means eloquent.[121] Rather, eloquence in speech is assured only to those who practice it carefully and regularly for a long period of time. In a passage which echoes Aristotle's *Categories*, John remarks that "what is difficult when we first try it, becomes easier after assiduous practice, and once the rules for doing it are mastered, very easy, unless languor creeps in, through lack of use or carelessness, and impedes our efficiency."[122] Eloquence, like other sorts of knowledge, is not readily acquired or retained; the successful rhetorician must take care to monitor all his behavior during his formative stage, or must be closely watched by an experienced tutor. Usage assures that *scientia* will be deeply rooted rather than facile.

The *Metalogicon* consequently subscribes to John's general belief that philosophy, far from being an abstruse and purely contemplative discipline, properly belongs in a more concrete setting as a guide for human thought and conduct. Any philosophy that does not emphasize practical goals offends against the very nature of that wisdom which philosophers claim to love, in John's judgment. The wisdom that human beings seek by means of abstract contemplation remains rooted in sense perception, that is, in the realm of *scientia,* which is the product of human action. Thus, no one can be wise except through learning based on practical experience. "By experience one acquires knowledge, which relates to action," the *Metalogicon* declares, so that man "derives the various rivulets of the sciences and wisdom from the fountainhead of sense perception."[123] This empirical foundation suggests, in effect, that the path to wisdom begins with the practice of particular acts, leading to the creation of a definite disposition of the soul toward knowledge. Once the individual is firmly in possession of knowledge (the prerequisite of wisdom), the powers of reason and understanding lead him toward the fruits of wisdom. No branch of learning that neglects this practical route to wisdom is deserving of the name of knowledge.[124] In sum, the pedagogical theory of the *Metalogicon* prefers experience to rote learning on the grounds that training by way of diligent application points the way that the wise man must follow. This Aristotelian premise provides a philosophical foundation for the claim that action and wisdom, so far from being incommensurable, are necessarily intertwined and indeed inseparable elements in the growth of human intellect.

Another dimension of John's practical bent in the *Metalogicon* stems from his insistence that education has a definite ethical component that requires recognition and examination. As he acknowledges in his prefatory remarks to the *Metalogicon,* "I have purposely incorporated into this treatise some observations concerning morals, since I am convinced that all good things read or written are

---

[121] *Metalogicon,* 165.

[122] *Metalogicon,* 30; cf. Aristotle, *Categories* 13a23–31.

[123] *Metalogicon,* 156–57.

[124] *Metalogicon,* 69.

useless except insofar as they have a good influence on one's manner of life. Any pretext of philosophy that does not bear fruit in the cultivation of virtue and the guidance of one's conduct is futile and false."[125] Making men virtuous is not a distinct enterprise from making them intelligent or knowledgeable; it is of no value to be well educated if one is unable to apply this learning in the service of moral rectitude. Moreover, the very techniques one employs in the acquisition of knowledge are subject to ethical evaluation and judgment. Proper learning is not defined merely by the quantity of the knowledge inculcated, but also by the quality of the educational experience. Specifically, John believes that the doctrine of moderation and the virtuous mean that he upholds in the *Policraticus* is also essential to any pedagogy which takes seriously its duty to mold morals as well as intellect.

The theme of moderation appears most prominently in the *Metalogicon*'s discussion of the correct attitude that the student ought to adopt toward his subject matter. In general, John advocates the principle that people must find a middle ground between an absence of intellectual curiosity and an overzealous pursuit of all topics. Intellectual discipline, John feels, arises out of adherence to a mean course between excess and defect: "Once we go beyond the proper limits, everything works in reverse, and excessive subtlety devours utility."[126] One should strive always in one's studies to exercise a vigilance that "tempers them lest anything become excessive."[127] What this means in large measure is that the intellect ought not to wander into those regions that are inappropriate to it. On the one hand, the mind must discriminate among its potential subjects of study in order to eliminate those that are unsuited to it, namely, matters that pertain to God alone as well as "whatever is noxious, such as images that encourage melancholy, anger and lust, or their daughters, envy, hate, calumny, luxury, and vanity." Yet, on the other hand, excessive caution yields an intellect that resists inquiry into new or foreign territory at all. Should the mind be inclined to be "overly cautious, it risks becoming timid, whereas if it grows too incautious, it is in peril of becoming foolhardy."[128] John thus maintains that proper philosophical investigation demands careful reflection upon the boundaries of one's intelligence, so as not to thrust oneself "temerariously and rashly into questions that exceed comprehension."[129] There are some topics with which the human mind is unprepared to deal, and to inquire after these is to court danger in the present world and in the afterlife. Nonetheless, John does not wish to discourage the correct application of the powers of reason. It is just as wrong to waste those capacities that God has granted by permitting them to atrophy as it is to presume that intellectual prowess bestows carte blanche to seek after any subject at all.

It is well enough to say that moderation should be the guide in planning and pursuing one's intellectual instruction. But how does this precept apply to

---

[125] *Metalogicon*, 11.
[126] *Metalogicon*, 67.
[127] *Metalogicon*, 155.
[128] *Metalogicon*, 149.
[129] *Metalogicon*, 181.

pedagogical practice? It is fortunate that John filled the *Metalogicon* with relevant examples of the usefulness of moderation in education. In the first place, John believes that a moderate attitude towards study is manifested in the very extent of the materials one consults. The *Metalogicon* warns that "to study everything that everyone, no matter how insignificant, has ever said, is either to be excessively humble and cautious, or overly vain and ostentatious."[130] The well-trained scholar will survey those authorities who are deserving of respect, but ignore works that do not merit effort and attention. Another consequence of the principle of moderation as used by John is that learning ought not to be an all-consuming and exclusive way of life. Those scholars who are unable to turn their minds to other pursuits manifest the weakness of their educations by exceeding the mean. How much better it is that "study should be moderated by recreation, so that while one's natural ability waxes strong with the former, it may be refreshed by the latter. . . .While innate ability proceeds from nature, it is fostered by use and sharpened by moderate exercise, but it is dulled by excessive work."[131] Constant study is a hindrance, rather than a boon, to the intellect. The overzealous scholar, no less than the too enthusiastic prince or prelate, courts counterproductive conduct if not the peril of his soul.

Even in the classroom, the doctrine of the mean has an appropriate role. As we have already discovered in examining John's account of knowledge, a thorough education rests largely on accustoming "one's students to practice the art they are studying." Such practice, however, can be taken to excess. The exercise of the learner's faculties, especially when done publicly in the presence of other students, should be pursued only "provided that charity regulates enthusiasm."[132] The patience of the instructor will bear fruit if he does not expect too great an improvement from his students too rapidly. Practice must be steady and slow as well as regular and extensive.

The notion that wisdom entails a moderate cast of mind appears to form the basis for John's criticism of pedagogical techniques current in the schools of his own day. "Anyone who makes an effort to be moderate in word and action," the *Metalogicon* complains, "is judged to have hidden motives."[133] In this regard, John feels that the classroom is no different from the royal court; the temper of the times discourages observation of the mean. Thus, instructors prompt students to all manner of intellectual excess. Disputations are conducted "at all times, in all places, and on all topics," in spite of the fact that "the excesses of those who think dialectical discussion consists in unbridled loquacity should have been restrained by Aristotle." It is on grounds of immoderation that John objects to the unrestrained use of the verbal duel: "The tongue of man . . . throws our life into confusion, and, unless it is checked by the reins of moderation, it hurls our entire person into the abyss." [134] He has observed this situation, he says, at first

---

[130] *Metalogicon*, 53.
[131] *Metalogicon*, 31.
[132] *Metalogicon*, 54.
[133] *Metalogicon*, 9.
[134] *Metalogicon*, 68–69.

hand. Given the opportunity to visit with his old associates from school days, and to gauge the progress of their thought, John reports that he came away sorely disappointed. Over the years, these former companions had acquired no greater wisdom and had benefited not at all from the potential fruits of philosophy. Indeed, "they had changed in but one regard: they had unlearned moderation; they no longer knew restraint."[135] Precisely for this reason, the *Metalogicon* urges re-evaluation of the contemporary practices associated with philosophical studies. When logic and dialectic are employed without any regard for the pursuit of wisdom, when their practice moves beyond the mean, they will be sterile and pointless. The path to wisdom, which philosophy purports to chart, demands that philosophers recognize the limitations of their own techniques and methods. When philosophy becomes immoderately fond of its own image, the goal of wisdom ceases to be paramount.

It should be evident, then, that the philosophy of the *Metalogicon* represents less a virtuoso technical performance than a rousing defense of the reflective life as it was propounded by the best of the schoolmen with whom John studied. Christopher Brooke's judgment that John's thought was simply a "mirror" of its age (meaning, implicitly, the product of a second-rate mind) seems too harsh.[136] Rather more fitting is K. S. B. Keats-Rohan's conclusion that John's general approach to philosophy shares important common properties with Cicero rather than with the technicians of the schools because he preferred to tackle ethical problems with a "clear-headed and commonsense attitude" that did not fit comfortably with many masters of the liberal arts and theology.[137] John's was a style of philosophy that was largely out of vogue in the schools of his time, as in ours today. That he could recognize and respect the value of a scholastic education, and defend it against its critics of various stripes, yet at the same time chastise teachers for their excesses and failings, demonstrates his sense of proportion and balance. John's philosophical commitment to moderation restrained him from any form of fanaticism and led him to embrace the philosophical ideals of the moderately skeptical New Academic. His turn to logical probability is unphilosophical only to those who adopt an ultra-doctrinaire insistence upon absolute certainty and rigid conceptual conformism in all intellectual matters. The *Metalogicon* rejects the latter as unworthy of the mantle of philosophy, and in so doing proves that its author does anything but "mirror" his environment. John indeed stands at considerable philosophical distance from many of the main currents of the mid-twelfth-century terrain.

John's principles of philosophical inquiry should thus be viewed in the context of his broadly humanistic project, namely, the identification of the features conducive to human happiness. Education is to be valued because knowledge and its byproducts (including social order and virtue) promote the earthly *summum bonum* of humanity. Like Cornificius, perhaps, John proposes a utilitarian

---

[135] *Metalogicon*, 73.

[136] Christopher Brooke, "John of Salisbury and His World," in *WJS*, 1–2.

[137] K. S. B. Keats-Rohan, "John of Salisbury and Education in Twelfth-Century Paris from the Account of His *Metalogicon*," *History of Universities* 6 (1986): 21.

criterion for the judgment of learning. In contrast to his nemesis, however, John's measure of useful knowledge is not the physical well-being associated with wealth, power, status, and luxury. Rather, he proposes that education, properly attained, promotes the useful goods of wisdom and virtue, qualities of the human soul that ultimately generate the highest degree of happiness. We should desire to be learned, John believes, because we will thereby fulfill our natural (and divinely ordained) purpose as human beings. And when we flourish in this way, we cannot fail to become happy in the way God intended. The *Metalogicon* is meant to be a guidebook to such happiness, a goal that John regards to be of far greater worth and far more befitting the philosopher than the technical pursuits too commonly found in the schools.

Historia Pontificalis

The years immediately following John's period of greatest intellectual output during the 1150s were relatively fallow, as the demands on his time occasioned by the wasting illness of Archbishop Theobald confined his writing to letters, so far as we know. His next (and final) major attempt to tackle a more reflective topic came during the time of his exile in France beginning in 1163, with the composition of the *Historia Pontificalis*. It is a slender volume of no more than 15,000 words; its uncompleted condition does not seem to have been the result of lost sections of manuscript but of John's abandonment of the task. The *Historia Pontificalis* is, as Christopher Brooke concludes, "a fragment."[138]

Characterizing this work is no easier than classifying John's previous writings. Addressed to Peter of Celle, the *Historia Pontificalis* purports simply to be an extension of the chronicle of Gembloux that had covered the history of the medieval church up to 1148.[139] But the work lacks the conventional qualities typical of medieval historical narrative, such as a chronological recounting of events from a "universal" perspective. It jumps across time and place during a three- or four-year period, at times indulging in long digressions about topics of presumably mutual interest to John and Peter. Sometimes it recounts important events, but often it records fairly obscure and minor incidents in considerable detail. This is not simply naïveté on John's part, an inability to distinguish between the major and the insignificant occurrences of his time. Rather, it reflects his own agenda in writing a work of history.

Like all of John's reflective writings, the *Historia Pontificalis* is at one and the same time both intensely personal and intellectually powerful: it brings its author's unique humanist perspective to bear on affairs of church, state, and school. Indeed, the book may constitute an especially intimate portrait of John's mind, since it does not seem to have been composed for any audience beyond

---

[138] Christopher Brooke, "Aspects of John of Salisbury's *Historia Pontificalis*," in *Intellectual Life in the Middle Ages*, ed. Lesley Smith and Benedicta Ward (London: Hambledon Press, 1992), 185–95, here 185.

[139] *Historia Pontificalis*, 2–4.

that of his close friend, Peter. The facts that it was left unfinished, exists in only a single manuscript, does not seem to have acquired much of a readership later in the Middle Ages, and remained unattributed to John until the nineteenth century, all reinforce the impression that it was intended as a work of private consolation during its author's French exile. John's works meant for more public consumption were highly polished and clearly subjected to revision and refinement. One does not have the same sense about the *Historia Pontificalis*.

This is not to imply that the treatise lacks sophistication. On the contrary, it carries forward in very conscious fashion many of John's favorite intellectual themes and methods. Admittedly, its use of classical quotations and allusions is more restrained than in John's other writings, reflective perhaps of the quality of the library to which he enjoyed access at Rheims. In addition to scripture, he cites Roman poets (Virgil, Ovid, Horace, Terence) and the Latin Fathers (Augustine, Jerome, Hilary) occasionally. He clearly had before him either a full copy of Gilbert of Poitiers's commentary on Boethius's *De Trinitate* or his own notes about it, since he presents a careful and detailed summary of that work.[140] But the most important source of all, John tells us in the preface, is "what I myself have seen and heard and know to be true, or else what credible men (*probabilium virorum*) have written and on supported authority."[141] As Roger Ray has pointed out, the deployment of the language of probability in this preface is not merely coincidental; it directly echoes the references to probable knowledge and the doctrines of the New Academy that appear in the prefaces to both the *Policraticus* and *Metalogicon*.[142] John signals that we have stepped into familiar intellectual territory, the realms of logical probability and moderate skepticism (associated with, in particular, Abelard and Cicero) that he explored in preceding tomes.

Nor should an essential continuity with John's earlier thought be surprising. The writing of history, it ought not be forgotten, was classified during the Middle Ages (as in classical times) as a branch of rhetoric. The *Historia Pontificalis* bears the marks of a work finely attuned to the rhetorical context of historical study. In Ray's estimation, the "great methodological premise of the *Historia Pontificalis*" is that "all who talk about particular human affairs, the rhetorician's exclusive field, trade in verisimilitude, not truth."[143] This precept is derived from the textbooks of classical rhetoric to which John had access, which taught that the rhetorician cannot expect to present the full truth; that is not his function. The rhetorical dimension of the *Historia Pontificalis* helps to explain what some scholars have simply considered to be John's even-handed and balanced treatment of the characters and events that he covers. John seems to adopt

[140] *Historia Pontificalis*, 28–41.

[141] *Historia Pontificalis*, 4.

[142] Roger Ray, "Rhetorical Skepticism and Verisimilar Narrative in John of Salisbury's *Historia Pontificalis*," in *Classical Rhetoric and Medieval Historiography*, ed. Ernst Breisach (Kalamazoo: Medieval Institute Publications, 1985), 61–102, here 77.

[143] Ray, "Rhetorical Skepticism and Verisimilar Narrative in John of Salisbury's *Historia Pontificalis*," 66.

an uncommitted attitude toward some individuals about whom elsewhere (for example, in correspondence) he expresses strong opinions.

On this score, the rhetorical background converges with elements of Abelardian probabilistic logic. Just as in John's earlier works, where it was proposed that the "free will" and independent judgment of rational minds were to decide questions open to legitimate doubt, so in the *Historia Pontificalis* he adopts a "sic et non" approach to his subject matter. Hence we hear about the good and the bad points of Pope Eugenius III, Bernard of Clairvaux, Henry of Blois, Bishop Godfrey of Langres—even the trouble-making Arnold of Brescia and John's own dear master Gilbert of Poitiers. John defers final judgment on such figures, even as he leaves a distinct impression about his own views. Since so much of his information, he admits, is based only on "probable" witnesses, he would be remiss in claiming as true knowledge what may only logically be supposed. The probabilities may suggest that the reader of the *Historia Pontificalis* should form one conclusion or another, but John refuses to assert for himself a monopoly on historical truth. Presumably, John would say that God alone possesses the competence to make ultimate determinations about the moral worth of human acts.

Nonetheless, John's very choice of subject matter hints that he wishes to employ the *Historia Pontificalis* to grind a personal axe or two and perhaps settle some old scores. His devotion to Archbishop Theobald—perhaps the only person discussed in the book who is treated in a wholly positive light—is particularly evident. The archbishop's courageous defiance of King Stephen's prohibition of his attendance at the Council of Rheims, his plea to Pope Eugenius for mercy on behalf of the English church, and his own forgiveness of the bishops who opposed him—all events of which John could claim direct knowledge—are held out as models of wise leadership. Any comparison of Theobald with other ecclesiastical lords is left to the reader, but seems implied. Where a powerful cleric such as Bernard of Clairvaux appeared only too ready to oppress and harass his fellow churchmen, Theobald's instinct was to forbear and absolve. Such implicit contrast, too, is a well-known technique of classical rhetoric.

It is also difficult to overlook John's expression of strong sympathy for Gilbert of Poitiers and of deep loathing for Arnulf of Lisieux. The very fact that he includes such a long digression, amounting to more than a quarter of the book, surveying the trial and teachings of Gilbert demonstrates his continued loyalty to a favored and long-dead teacher.[144] The presentation of Gilbert as an honest, thoughtful, and above all orthodox individual, undeserving of the victimization he endured, would surely not have sat well with the clerics who in the 1160s were pursuing the cause of Bernard of Clairvaux's canonization (which finally occurred in 1174). Perhaps this affords another reason why John kept the text of the *Historia Pontificalis* out of public circulation. As for Arnulf, who is depicted (unfairly, some think) as a greedy thug, John can barely hide his contempt. Arnulf stands accused of letting self-interest take precedence over duty, leading to

---

[144] *Historia Pontificalis*, 15–41.

the collapse of the Second Crusade.[145] John also presents Arnulf as the hench-
man of King Stephen—one villain who makes no direct appearance in the *Historia Pontificalis*, but who hovers in the background—in his efforts to crown his
son, Eustace. Into Arnulf's mouth is placed a declaration before Pope Innocent
in 1139 denouncing Countess Matilda as illegitimate and not entitled to inherit
the throne of England. To this John counters a speech by Archbishop Ulger of
Angers which labels the bishop of Lisieux as impudent, mendacious, and treach-
erous, while refuting the charges made against the empress.[146] Since John was
manifestly not present at these events, and since an eyewitness report states that
Ulger in fact made no reply to the charges,[147] we may presume the latter speech
to be a product of the author's imagination, yet another opportunity to denounce
his enemy, the evidence notwithstanding. In the instances of both Gilbert and
Arnulf, then, John shades his presentation to reflect his personal stake in the
historical narrative. Inasmuch as his presumed audience of one, Peter of Celle,
was all too familiar with this background, the poignancy of the accounts would
have occurred to him immediately.

Perhaps the most surprising element of the *Historia Pontificalis*, given its title, is the absence of much discussion of the pope or the papacy. The pope whose
court is at the center of the book, Eugenius, remains largely a cipher whose most
notable acts involve the reconciliation of married couples who had desired the
nullification of their marriages (and even in this enterprise, he did not prove ultimately successful).[148] The closest John comes to an evaluation of Eugenius is a
sort of rebuke (couched in familiar probabilistic fashion) concerning the fre-
quency with which the pope's decisions were later countermanded. John specu-
lates about the reasons for this, which are attributed variously to flaws of character and poor advice.[149] It is evident that, whatever rationale John may have had
for choosing the events of the Council of Rheims and its aftermath as his object
of historical narrative, an abiding respect for the accomplishments of Eugenius's
pontificate is not among them. Again, a comparison with Theobald, whose negotiations with King Stephen and the lords of the English church recur throughout
the text, may reasonably be inferred. The Archbishop of Canterbury displays a
strength of character and vision of purpose that seem absent in the pope.

On the other hand, nothing in the *Historia Pontificalis* suggests that John
rates the pontificate of Eugenius as a failure. It was an orderly period for the
church, even amid the disaster of the Second Crusade: kings were largely deferential to papal authority, and the business of the church was conducted for the
most part tranquilly. The apparently unexceptional character of Eugenius's rule
may mask precisely the point that John wishes to make. In the *Policraticus*, he
had emphasized in connection with secular power that a prince's rule is to be
judged worthy even if he does no great good, provided that he does no great evil

---

[145] *Historia Pontificalis*, 54–56.
[146] *Historia Pontificalis*, 83–85.
[147] See Brooke, "Aspects of John of Salisbury's *Historia Pontificalis*," 186.
[148] *Historia Pontificalis*, 61–62, 80–82.
[149] *Historia Pontificalis*, 51.

and ensures that his subjects behave with restraint.[150] One wonders whether such a principle may not also stand behind his analysis of papal government. In particular, the contrast with the 1160s—with the papal schism and the attacks on the church from both German and English rulers—may not have been far from John's mind. The *Historia Pontificalis* is open to interpretation as a portrayal of how the church may still operate effectively and fruitfully even when its head possesses no especially preeminent or superlative qualities.

The *Historia Pontificalis* ought to be read, then, not merely as an adjunct to John's other writings, but as a concrete application of his most cherished intellectual principles of rhetoric, logic, ethics, and politics to the "facts" of history. It is a work that merits a place alongside the rest of his major texts, even though it lacks some of the final polish of the *Metalogicon* or *Policraticus*. John takes his greatly vaunted union of philosophical wisdom and practical reason into a world that he knows all too well, the realm of the ecclesiastical court. He reveals, in particular, the traps and snares to which courtiers are constantly exposed and highly susceptible. The *Historia Pontificalis* may thus hint at some of the reasons why John felt compelled in 1164 to announce his formal withdrawal from the court of Canterbury and retirement from public life. Even in relatively stable and harmonious times, it is too easy for good men (Gilbert and Theobald, for instance) to find themselves abused and downtrodden by the powerful figures of church and state. Of course, John's own retreat was temporary: the clearly tyrannical intransigence of King Henry II and his supporters constituted such an affront that, as a man of honor and religion, he could not refuse re-engagement in Archbishop Thomas Becket's cause.

Miscellaneous and Spurious Writings

In addition to the main writings already surveyed, John of Salisbury's extant corpus includes about three hunded and twenty-five genuine letters, a *Vita Anselmi*, and the *Vita et Passio Sancti Thome*. Moreover, John's modern editors, at least through the middle of the nineteenth century, attributed to him two further works—a 200-line poem entitled *De Membris Conspirantibus* and a neo-Platonic treatise called *De Septem Septenis*—as well as a number of other letters, the authorship of which is disputable.[151] Although these texts do not command or merit the same attention as John's four major treatises, some comment may be appropriate regarding their place in the body of his literary output.

The spuria may be dismissed with relative ease. Christopher Brooke explains clearly the reasons why he eliminated several items that had in confusion previously been included with John's correspondence.[152] The ascription of *De Membris Conspirantibus* to John resulted from a passing remark by one of his early modern editors about its resemblance to some of the leading ideas of his

---

[150] Keats-Rohan, 265.

[151] John of Salisbury, *Opera Omnia*, ed. J. A. Giles (Oxford: J. H. Parker, 1848), v. 5. These attributions were adopted in PL 199, where the works are printed as John's.

[152] *Letters*, 2:809.

other works, in particular the tale of the revolt of the limbs and organs against the stomach in *Policraticus* Book 6, Chapter 24. But this metaphorical story was a popular one, widely recounted during antiquity and the Middle Ages. Indeed, another twelfth-century poetic version of it has been attributed to the pen of Marie de France.[153] Its most recent editor, Ronald Pepin, points out that no proof of any sort exists to support John's authorship of *De Membris Conspirantibus*.[154]

Somewhat less explicable is the identification of John's hand behind *De Septem Septenis*, a twelfth-century Neoplatonic treatise that has been implicated in the development of medieval Hermeticism.[155] Giles printed the tract for the first time in his 1848 *Opera Omnia* without explanation,[156] and on that basis it was included in the John of Salisbury volume of the *Patrologia Latina*. But Carl Schaarschmidt decisively rejected John's authorship of it only a few years later.[157] The tract, which purports to identify the seven principles of cosmological knowledge in self-consciously Hermetic terms, bears no tangible relation to any of John's other writings and rightly deserves to be excised from his corpus.

Among John's genuine writings, his hagiographies do not stand out as shining examples of the genre. The *Vita Anselmi*, written in support of Becket's unsuccessful effort to achieve Anselm of Canterbury's canonization in 1163, is mostly derivative of the famous *Vita* by Eadmer.[158] While he supplies a few details about Anselm's career that Eadmer neglects, John sets aside his rhetorical and literary skills in favor of a relatively straightforward narrative of its subject's career. Only a single manuscript of John's life exists,[159] in comparison with the many copies of Eadmer's version. It has been demonstrated that a poetic version of the life of Anselm (bound into the same volume as John's text) probably written before 1170 constitutes a "versified epitome of the prose life by John of Salisbury,"[160] but the treatise does not seem to have gained any wider audience in later times.

The *Vita et Passio Sancti Thome* must likewise be counted among John's less significant works. The rather perfunctory treatment of Becket's career and character suggests that its composition was rather hasty; it was, after all, meant as a preface to a letter collection, not as a full hagiography in its own right. The

[153] Cary J. Nederman and Kate Langdon Forhan, eds., *Readings in Medieval Political Theory, 1100–1400* (Indianapolis: Hackett Publishers, 2000), 24–25.

[154] Ronald E. Pepin, " 'On the Conspiracy of the Members,' Attributed to John of Salisbury," *Allegorica* 12 (1991): 29–31.

[155] See, most recently, Robert Ziomkowski, "Science, Theology, and Myth in Medieval Creationism: Cosmogony in the Twelfth Century" (Ph.D. Diss. Department of History, Cornell University, 2000), Chap. 5.

[156] *Opera Omnia*, ed. Giles, 5:209–38.

[157] Carl Schaarschmidt, *Johannes Saresberiensis* (Leipzig: B.G. Teubner, 1862), 278–81.

[158] Eadmer, *The Life of Saint Anselm, Archbishop of Canterbury*, ed. R. W. Southern (London: Thomas Nelson and Sons, 1962).

[159] Eadmer, *The Life of Saint Anselm*, xxiv.

[160] D. J. Sheerin, "An Anonymous Verse Epitome of the Life of St. Anselm," *Analecta Bollandiana* 92 (1974): 114.

most compelling part of the *Vita* is the account of Thomas's death, but this is derived directly from John's letter of early 1171 to John of Canterbury describing the events (and recall that he had fled the scene, so large segments of his report were second-hand). In spite of Stephen Jaeger's recent attempt to implicate the *Vita et Passio Sancti Thome* in the general spirit of "moral philosophy" that imbued other contemporary biographies of the martyr,[161] John's effort pales before the version of Herbert of Bosham. Why John failed to bring his substantial literary talents to bear on a story so dramatic and with which he was closely associated remains a mystery that could be solved only if much more were to be known about his circumstances in the early 1170s.

Fortunately, John's two letter collections afford a far better illustration of his intellectual and literary powers. His nineteenth-century editor, Giles, felt that "the Epistolary writings" constituted his "most important work."[162] Later scholars have not been quite so enthusiastic, but they have certainly recognized that John's letters are not merely historical artifacts. Peter of Celle remarks to John (apparently about the first collection) upon the erudition and beauty of their composition, not to mention the wisdom that they contain.[163] The first collection, comprising one hundred and thirty-five letters, is heavily weighted toward documenting the everyday work of administration at Canterbury. Nearly three-quarters of the letters contained therein were sent under Archbishop Theobald's signature to the papal court, the king, and the various jurisdictions and leaders within the English church. For the most part, this set of correspondence renders Canterbury's opinions on matters of law, states the basis of appeal to the papacy, and explicates to the royal court the reasons behind the archbishop's determinations. These letters leave the impression of John as a busy, multi-competent, and thorough clerical administrator whose devotion to the liberty and primacy of Canterbury was tempered only by his high regard for and deference to the authority of Rome. Taken as a whole, the Theobald correspondence authored by John provides a useful model of the well-ordered church curia in action on the larger stage of ecclesiastical and secular politics.

The remaining thirty-seven personal letters contained in the first collection display more of the literary attributes that one might expect of John. These missives are mainly addressed to three individuals with whom he enjoyed especially close relationships: Peter of Celle, John of Canterbury (now treasurer of York), and Pope Adrian IV (formally Cardinal Nicholas Brakespear). In writing to his intimates, John draws upon his vast learning in classical and scriptural sources and employs a style of expression reminiscent of the great Latin epistolary authors (pagans such as Seneca and Cicero, as well as Christians such as Augustine) who seem to have furnished his model. The language is witty, filled with puns and playful turns of phrase; the contents are also sometimes brutally honest in the evaluation of certain people for whom the author had low regard. The missives seem intent upon upholding a paradigm of literary friendship

---

[161] Jaeger, *The Envy of Angels*, 297–309.

[162] *Opera Omnia*, ed. Giles, 3:v.

[163] See *Letters*, 1:x–xi.

founded upon the international community of letters.[164] As John says in a letter to Peter, "Since I have professed myself to be your friend, I gladly acknowledge our partnership of mind and possessions."[165] John's personal correspondence embodies an ideal of Latin literacy that could unite men of widely differing nationalities, ranks, and responsibilities into a fellowship of Christian intellectuals devoted to sharing their learning and applying it to everyday affairs.

Generally, John's letters tend to be composed as the situation permits, in particular when he encounters a traveler at court who is heading to the location of a friend. Thus he is forced to reply often to jibes from his correspondents about his poor record of writing, the press of business for Canterbury and the lack of a reliable go-between being his regular excuses. Not surprisingly, the single most concentrated body of personal communications comes during the period of Henry II's displeasure with John in 1156–1157, when he has been prevented from undertaking many of his duties on behalf of the archbishop. In a series of letters, John narrates to Peter primarily, but also to Pope Adrian and others, his circumstances, and commences his meditations on fortune that were to take shape as he began to write the work of consolation that would become the *Policraticus*.[166]

For the most part, John's early correspondence, while self-reflective, is not especially philosophical in content. A rare exception is the letter he sends to Peter in late 1159 on the occasion of the conveyance of the newly completed *Policraticus* for his friend's comments. John's accompanying missive announces much of the conceptual structure that holds the book together. He articulates, in particular, how the good order of the natural world stems from its organization as a totality in which all phenomena "derive their strength from mutual aid." The universe is structured according to an "indwelling spirit of unanimity" that "nurtures the concord of things dissident and the dissidence of things concordant." The physical world forms a whole whose dissimilar parts cooperate in order to produce a singular result, since the spirit of unanimity "arranges the diverse parts of the universe as though they were its members, in order that they may be attuned for mutual and reciprocal service."[167] This principle John observes to be at work also in the human body, and it forms the basis, of course, for the organic metaphor that he details in Books 5 and 6 of the *Policraticus*. Similar ideas also pervade the *Metalogicon*'s discussion of human society and the bonds of civilization. The letter thus illuminates a central tenet of John's philosophical thought and ought to be read as a supplement to his other treatises.

John's second collection of letters, dating from 1163 through the early 1170s, has noteworthy differences that demarcate it from its predecessor in several ways. Of the nearly one hundred and seventy-five letters that form the core

---

[164] Giles Constable, *Letters and Letter Collections*, Typologie des sources du moyen âge occidental 17 (Turnhout: Brepols, 1976).

[165] *Letters*, 1:180 (Letter 111).

[166] *Letters*, 1:31–34 (Letters 19, 21), 44–46 (Letters 27 and 28), 48–55 (Letters 30–33).

[167] *Letters*, 1:181 (Letter 111).

of the compilation, all were written under his own name, with the exceptions of one missive each that he drafted on behalf of Peter of Celle and Thomas Becket.[168] (This is not counting another fifteen or so letters authored after 1173, several of which were composed on behalf of Exeter or Canterbury.) It remains possible, however, to distinguish between those letters that are entirely professional and those that are of a more personal nature. Into the former category fall the many epistles John produced in defense of the cause of Becket, especially after the middle of 1166 when he concluded that it was necessary to throw his support wholeheartedly behind the archbishop. (Fewer than twenty letters can be dated with certainty to the period between the first item in 1164 and John's disastrous meeting with Henry II in the spring of 1166.) These letters are generally addressed to high authorities in the church, including Pope Alexander III and clerical officials throughout France and England, with the intent of developing strategies for achieving Becket's settlement with Henry or of admonishing people who seemed to be favoring the cause of the English crown over that of the archbishop. Such letters are particularly useful for assessing the course of the dispute and the shifting political alliances that shaped the events leading up to December 1170. Perhaps more broadly, they testify to conditions opposite to those found in the "professional" correspondence dating to Theobald's time. They portray a church in disarray, besieged by the secular rulers and clerics who have placed base interests above their duties to God.

Into the class of "personal" correspondence may be assigned letters to familiars that relate John's private fears, concerns, and wishes as well as conveying advice to fellow supporters of Canterbury about how to proceed. They are also full of rumor, gossip, and the latest news of events in England and on the continent. Becket himself was the recipient of many of these letters, as were old friends and associates such as John of Canterbury (now bishop of Poitiers), Bartholomew of Exeter, and Baldwin of Totnes. (There are no letters to Peter of Celle, of course, because John remained with his old friend at Rheims until his return to England in late 1170.) This group of communications shares some common features with the personal letters from the first collection, inasmuch as both draw upon John's skill as a writer and his talent for sophisticated literary allusion. But the second set of personal letters expresses much more overtly his humanist sensibilities and his philosophical predilections than does the earlier correspondence, if only because he had a great deal more time to ruminate than he did during the busy days as Theobald's secretary.

Some of the later letters, indeed, contain the most powerful statements of his humanism to be found anywhere in his corpus. To Gerard Pucelle, for instance, John writes in late 1166, "True philosophy seeks, attends to, and gains real things, not words; and you have long known that I have never approved of an opinion based on talk alone. Nor are mere hearers of the word, nor preachers of it, righteous in God's eyes, but doers." Virtue, he goes on to say, repels the assault of fate with action.[169] Here we encounter in brief the precept that guided John throughout

---

[168] *Letters*, 2:28–31 (Letter 143), 64–67 (Letter 157).
[169] *Letters*, 2:224–25 (Letter 185).

the period of his exile: the man of honor and religion must be prepared to demonstrate his character by conducting himself in a manner consistent with his cherished principles, regardless of consequence. To another friend, John Saracen, he gives thanks for exile and outlawry, since this apparent misfortune has in fact afforded a decisive test of his virtue and permitted him to enter more comfortably into the company of philosophers.[170] Similar remarks about learning the lessons of philosophy "the hard way" are widely scattered throughout the letters from the 1160s.

In the second collection of letters, John also demonstrates that philosophy has a role to play in the understanding and appraisal of historical occurrences. He deploys philosophical language and concepts originally articulated in his work of the 1150s in order to analyze events and personal characteristics connected with the Becket conflict. For instance, the greatly vaunted quality of moderation forms a central theme of John's correspondence, appearing in his appraisal of the principals to the dispute, each of whom he criticizes at one or another time for acting excessively. A missive addressed by him to John of Canterbury observes that King Henry II would enjoy universal praise and acclaim "if he would only defer more to the church of God, and act more moderately with those who reason with him, and inhibit his language and spirit from outbreaks of anger and other reprehensible emotions, according to the measure of royal dignity."[171] (Ironically, of course, it is precisely the immoderate royal temper that led indirectly to Becket's assassination.) Precisely on account of Henry's excessiveness, John tells Gerard Pucelle, the king needs to reconcile himself with Becket: "The archbishop of Canterbury will inspire the soul of the lord king to employ moderately his divine license."[172] John perceives Becket to be a counterbalance to Henry, since his absence from England has allowed the king to give full play to his tyrannical tendencies. John's correspondence regularly styles Henry a "tyrant,"[173] a term that in the usage of the *Policraticus* means a ruler who employs his power excessively in order to suppress the liberty of his subjects. The true king rules within the bounds of moderation, always according a proper measure of freedom to those over whom he reigns. Henry demands an unwavering and unquestioning acceptance of his dictates that is incompatible with liberty. To Baldwin of Totnes, John comments, "It is the man's nature to make light of all the merits of one who for whatever reasons breaks or postpones obedience to a single mandate, no matter what it is. The 'moderation' of his requests . . . is such that it is sometimes necessary to disobey."[174] Henry's propensity toward excess in his conduct renders him morally unfit to govern his realm, as evidenced by his oppression of the liberty of the English church.

---

[170] *Letters*, 2:270–71 (Letter 194).

[171] *Letters*, 2:634–35 (Letter 287).

[172] *Letters*, 2:686–87 (Letter 297).

[173] For instance, *Letters*, 2:237–38 (Letter 187), 429–30 (Letter 234), 455–58 (Letter 239).

[174] *Letters,* 2:468–69 (Letter 241).

More surprising than John's condemnation of Henry's character is the doubt expressed in the letters, particularly those written before the middle of 1166, about the immoderate qualities of Becket's personality. John displays an acute awareness of the archbishop's defects, which he ascribes to a tendency to exceed moderate bounds. To Humphrey Bos, John bluntly states, "I have kept the faith owed to the church and archbishop of Canterbury, and I have stood by him faithfully in England and on the continent when justice and moderation seemed to be his. If he ever seemed to detour from justice or exceed the mean, I stood up to him to his face."[175] Becket shows little sense of discretion with regard to judgments of circumstance, John observes, telling Bartholomew, "He who inspects our hearts and judges our words and acts knows that I—more than any other mortal—have upbraided the lord archbishop on the grounds that he has from the beginning inadvisedly provoked the resentment of the king and court by his zeal, since many provisions should have been made for place and time and persons."[176] In other words, during the earliest stages of the dispute between king and archbishop, John held the latter as well as the former responsible: two immoderate men confronted one another without regard for propriety. Even once John had been forced to commit himself entirely to Becket's cause, he could not resist counseling a moderate course for the archbishop. In July 1166, John, fearing his master's propensity toward rash behavior, exhorted him to display virtuous moderation in his negotiations with his opponents. "It is especially expedient that your moderation be known to all," John recommends, "With moderation write and state the conditions [of a reconciliation], since it seems to be certain that the souls of the enemies of God's church are so hardened that they will admit no condition at all."[177] Hinting at the Ciceronian view that what is expedient and what is honorable are ultimately inseparable, John suggests that Becket position himself as a conciliatory figure, not an extremist. Whenever someone accuses Thomas of acting out of pride or hatred, rather than virtue and religious conviction, "this opinion should be answered by exhibiting moderation in deeds and words, in conduct and dress."[178] The archbishop is advised to imitate "the most modest David" in order that "you can moderately reply" to "those who reprove, indeed severely deride you."[179] John thus enunciates an unbreakable principle that should direct Becket: "In all things behave such that your moderation may be known by all. . . . Attend to the state of the times, the condition of the Roman church, the needs of the English realm."[180] This advice the archbishop largely chose to ignore, even after his return to England in December 1170. A more moderate Becket might have made a far less dramatic martyr, but he would also very likely have done less damage to either the church or the state in England.

---

[175] *Letters*, 2:20–23 (Letter 139).
[176] *Letters*, 2:48–49 (Letter 150).
[177] *Letters*, 2:168–69 (Letter 176).
[178] *Letters*, 2:170–71 (Letter 176).
[179] *Letters*, 2:172–73 (Letter 176).
[180] *Letters*, 2:190–91 (Letter 179).

Tracing the philosophical lineage of John's thought into his letters illustrates the essential unity of his intellectual perspective. He did not discriminate radically between his speculative and his practical work. On the contrary, he seems to have been enthusiastic about incorporating philosophical principles into the conduct of his everyday life as well as his analysis of contemporary events and personalities. Surely this represents one of the cornerstones of his humanism: he believed that philosophy had a crucial role in guiding human beings toward overcoming obstacles to their true happiness. Philosophy was not to be left at the schoolhouse door, for it ought to occupy an important place in the world at large. The task of philosophical discourse is to aid in discerning the good from the evil, the true from the false, and so to illuminate the path toward happiness by navigating the tricky by-ways of public life. John's devotion to the practical implications of abstract thought should indeed act as sufficient encouragement for philosophers and political theorists to examine more carefully his correspondence, as for political and ecclesiastical historians to pay closer attention to his philosophical doctrines. The life of the mind and the life of action were of a piece for John of Salisbury.

BIBLIOGRAPHY 1983–2004

In *The World of John of Salisbury*, published in 1984, David Luscombe compiled a comprehensive bibliography of works by and on John of Salisbury published between 1953 and 1982. In turn, Luscombe's bibliography supplemented a 1958 survey produced by H. Hohenleutner, which appeared in volume 77 of the *Historisches Jahrbuch der Görres-Gesellschaft* (1958). The present bibliography brings this work forward into the new millennium, and also adds some earlier items that were not present in the prior bibliographies. Helpful in accomplishing this task were the seven issues of the *John of Salisbury Newsletter* edited and published by Ronald E. Pepin between 1986 and 1992. I have included only work that contains substantive discussion of, and not merely passing reference to, John of Salisbury. The present bibliography has been organized topically, rather than chronologically (as in Luscombe), and the entries have been alphabetized within each topic. I have omitted citations to book reviews of editions of John of Salisbury's work or of writings about his life and thought.

Writings by John of Salisbury

Entheticus Maior et Minor. Ed. and trans. Jan van Laarhoven. 3 vols. Studien und Texte zur Geistesgeschichte des Mittelalters 17. Leiden: E.J. Brill, 1987.

Entheticus. Ed. and trans. Ronald E. Pepin. In *Allegorica* 9 (1987): 7–133.

Historia Pontificalis. Ed. Marjorie Chibnall. Rev. ed. Oxford Medieval Texts. Oxford: Oxford University Press, 1986.

Metalogicon. Ed. J. B. Hall and K. S. B Keats-Rohan. Corpus Christianorum Continuatio Medievalis 98. Turnhout: Brepols, 1991.

Policraticus I–IV. Ed. K. S. B. Keats-Rohan. Corpus Christianorum Continuatio Medievalis 117. Turnhout: Brepols, 1993. [*Policraticus V–VIII* has been announced but has yet to appear.]

Policraticus. Ed. Clement C.J. Webb. New intro. by Patricia McNulty. 2 vols. in 1. European Political Thought: Traditions and Endurance. Reprint ed. New York: Arno Press, 1979.

Policraticus Livres I–III. Trans. [1372] Denis Foulechat. Ed. Charles Bruckner. Publications Romanes et Françaises. Geneva: Librairie Droz, 1994.

Policraticus Livre IV. Trans. [1372] Denis Foulechat. Ed. Charles Bruckner. Travaux du C.R.A.L. 3. Nancy: Presses Universitaires de Nancy, 1985.

Policraticus. Ed. Miguel Angel Ladero. Trans. M. Alcalá. Clásicos para una Biblioteca Contemporánea. Madrid: Editora Nacional, 1984.

Policraticus [selections]. Ed. and trans. Maria Teresa Fumagalli Beoni-Brocchieri. Intro. Luca Bianchi. Biblioteca di cultura medievale, Di fronte e attraverso 137. Milan: Jaca Book, 1985.

Policraticus [selections]. Ed. and trans. Cary J. Nederman. Cambridge Texts in the History of Political Thought. Cambridge: Cambridge University Press, 1990, rev. ed. 1992.

Policraticus [selections]. Abridged and ed. Murray F. Markland. Milestones of Thought. New York: Frederick Ungar Publishing, 1979.

Vita Sancti Anselmi and *Vita Sancti Thomae*. In *Anselmo e Becket, due vite*, ed. I. Biffi. Milan: 1990.

Works on John of Salisbury: Life and Career

Barker, Lynn K. "MS Bodl. Canon. Pat. Lat. 131 and a Lost Lactantius of John of Salisbury: Evidence in Search of a French Critic of Thomas Becket." *Albion* 22 (1990): 21–37.

———. "Ecclesiology and the Twelfth-Century Church in the Letters of Peter of Celle." M.A. Thesis, Department of History, University of North Carolina at Chapel Hill, 1978.

Barlow, Frank. "John of Salisbury and His Brothers." *Journal of Ecclesiastical History* 46 (1995): 95–109.

Brooke, Christopher N.L. "Adrian IV and John of Salisbury." In *Adrian IV, The English Pope: Studies and Texts*, ed. Brenda Bolton and Anne J. Duggan, 1–12. Aldershot: Ashgate, 2002.

Duggan, Anne J. "Classical Quotations and Allusions in the Correspondence of Thomas Becket." *Viator* 32 (2001): 1–22.

Fryde, Natalie M. "The Roots of Magna Carta: Opposition to the Plantagenets." In *Political Thought and the Realities of Power in the Middle Ages*, ed. Joseph Canning and Otto Gerhard Oexle, 53–65. Göttingen: Vandenhoeck & Ruprecht, 1998.

Hirata, Yoko. "John of Salisbury, Gerard Pucelle, and *amicitia*." In *Friendship in Medieval Europe*, ed. Julian Haseldine, 153–65. Stroud: Sutton, 1999.

———. "John of Salisbury and Thomas Becket: The Making of a Martyr." *Medieval History* 2 (1992): 18–25.

Jeauneau, Edouard. "Jean de Salisbury et la lecture des philosophes." *Revue des Études Augustiniennes* 29 (1983): 145–74. [Also in *WJS*.]

Keats-Rohan, K. S. B. "John of Salisbury and Education in Twelfth-Century Paris from the Account of His *Metalogicon*." *History of Universities* 6 (1986): 1–45.

Laarhoven, Jan van. "*Non iam decreta, sed Evangelium!* Jean de Salisbury au Latran III." In *Dalla Chiesa antica alla Chiesa moderna: Miscellanea per il Cinquantesimo della Facoltà di Storia Ecclesiastica della Pontificia Università Gregoriana*, ed. Mario Fois, Vincenzo Monachino, and Felix Litva, 107–119. Miscellanea historiae pontificiae 50. Rome: Gregorian Pontifical University, 1987.

McGuire, Brian P. *Friendship and Community: The Monastic Experience 350–1250*. Kalamazoo: Cistercian Publications, 1988.

McLoughlin, John. "*Amicitia* in Practice: John of Salisbury (c.1120–1180) and his Circle." In *England in the Twelfth Century: Proceedings of the 1988 Harlaxton Symposium*, ed. D. Williams, 165–80. Woodbridge: Boydell & Brewer, 1990.

———. "Nations and Loyalties: The Outlook of a Twelfth-Century Schoolman (John of Salisbury, c.1120–1180)." In *Faith and Identity: Christian Political Experience*, ed. D. Loades and K. Walsh, 39–46. Studies in Church History Subsidia 6. Oxford: Blackwell, 1990.

———. "John of Salisbury (c. 1120–1180): The Career and Attitudes of a Schoolman in Church Politics." Ph.D. Dissertation, University College Dublin, 1988.

———. "The Language of Persecution: John of Salisbury and the Early Phase of the Becket Dispute." In *Persecution and Toleration*, ed. W. J. Shiels, 73–87. Studies in Church History 21. Oxford: Basil Blackwell, 1984.

Pepin, Ronald E. " 'On the Conspiracy of the Members,' Attributed to John of Salisbury." *Allegorica* 12 (1991): 29–41.

———. "*Amicitia Jocosa*: Peter of Celle and John of Salisbury." *Florilegium* 3 (1983): 140–56.

Southern, Richard W. *Scholastic Humanism and the Unification of Europe*, v. 2. Oxford: Blackwell, 2001.

———. "The Schools of Paris and the School of Chartres." In *Renaissance and Renewal in the Twelfth Century*, ed. Robert L. Benson and Giles Constable, 113–37. Cambridge, MA: Harvard University Press, 1982.

Zanoletti, Gabriella. *Il bello come vero alla Scuola di Chartres: Giovanni di Salisbury*. Rome: L. Lucarini, 1979.

Works on the Writings of John of Salisbury: General

Arduini, Maria Lodovica. " 'Sola Ratione' in Giovanni di Salisbury." *Rivista di Filosofia Neo-scolastica* 89 (1997): 229–66.

Boczar, Mieczysław. *Czlowiek i wspólnota: filozofia molna, spoleczna i polityczna Jana z Salisbury* [*Man and Community: The Moral, Social, and Political Philosophy of John of Salisbury*]. Warsaw: Wydawnictwa Uniwersytetu Warszawskiego, 1987.

———. "Koncepcja retoryki w pismach Jana z Salisbury" ("The Concept of Rhetoric in John of Salisbury's Writings"). *Kwartalnik Historii Nauki i Techniki* 32 (1987): 139–55.

———. " 'Ratio naturae et officii' w filozofii spolecznej Jana z Salisbury" [" 'Ratio naturae et officii' in the Social Philosophy of John of Salisbury"]. *Studia Mediewistyczne* 24 (1985): 3–28.

Brown, Catherine. *Contrary Things: Exegesis, Dialectic, and the Poetics of Didacticism*. Stanford: Stanford University Press, 1998.

Burnett, Charles. "John of Salisbury and Aristotle." *Didascalion* 2 (1998): 19–32.

Dotto, Gianni. *Giovanni di Salisbury: La filosofia come sapienza*. Assisi: Edizione Porziunco, 1986.

Ferruolo, Stephen C. *The Origins of the University: The Schools of Paris and Their Critics, 1100–1215*. Stanford: Stanford University Press, 1985.

Garfagnini, Gian Carlo. "L'attività storico-filosofica nel secolo XII: Giovanni di Salisbury." *Studi medievali* 3rd ser., 30 (1989): 839–53.

————. "Da Seneca a Giovanni di Salisbury: 'Auctoritates' morali e 'vitae philosophorum' in un Ms. Trecentesco." *Renascimento* 2nd ser., 20 (1980): 201–47.

Godman, Peter. *The Silent Masters: Latin Literature and Its Censors in the High Middle
Ages*. Princeton: Princeton University Press, 2000.

Hirata, Yoko. *Collected Papers on John of Salisbury and His Correspondents* [in Japa-
nese and English]. Tokyo: Hakuto Shubo, 1996.

Kerner, Max. "Johannes von Salisbury und das gelehrte Recht." In *Proceedings of the
Ninth International Congress of Medieval Canon Law*, ed. Peter Landau and
Joers Mueller, 503–21. Monumenta Iuris Canonici Subsidia 10. Vatican City:
Biblioteca Apostolica Vaticana, 1997.

Lounsbury, Richard C. "The Case of the Erudite Eyewitness: Cicero, Lucan, and John of
Salisbury." *Allegorica* 12 (1990): 15–35.

Michel, Alain. "Autour de Jean de Salisbury: La dignité humaine et l'honneur de Dieu."
In *Gli Umanesimi Medievali*, ed. Claudio Leonardi, 375–82. Florence: SIS-
MEL, Edizioni del Galluzzo, 1998.

Monagle, Clare. "Contested Knowledges: John of Salisbury's *Metalogicon* and *Historia
Pontificalis*." *Parergon* 21 (2004): 1–17.

————. "Bookish Heresy: The Trial of Gilbert of Poitiers and Its Narrations." M.A. Thesis, Department of History, Monash University, 1999.

Moos, Peter von. "Die angeslehre Meinung: Studien zum *endoxon* im Mittelalter IV:
Johann von Salisbury." *Mittellateinisches Jahrbuch* 34 (1999): 1–55.

Nederman, Cary J. *Worlds of Difference: European Discourses of Toleration, c.1100–
c.1550*, 39–52. University Park: Pennsylvania State University Press, 2000.

————. "Toleration, Skepticism, and the 'Clash of Ideas': Principles of Liberty in the
Writings of John of Salisbury." In *Beyond the Persecuting Society: Religious
Toleration Before the Enlightenment*, ed. John Christian Laursen and Cary J.
Nederman, 53–70. Philadelphia: University of Pennsylvania Press, 1998.

————. "Nature, Ethics, and the Doctrine of '*Habitus*': Aristotelian Moral Psychology in
the Twelfth Century." *Traditio* 45 (1989/1990): 87–110.

————. "The Changing Face of Tyranny: The Reign of King Stephen in the Political
Thought of John of Salisbury." *Nottingham Medieval Studies* 33 (1989): 1–20.

Nederman, Cary and Tsae Lan Lee Dow. "The Road to Heaven is Paved with Pious De-
ceptions: Medieval Speech Ethics and Deliberative Democracy." In *Talking
Democracy: Historical Approaches to Rhetoric and Democratic Theory*, ed.
Benedetto Fontana, Cary J. Nederman, and Gary Remer, 187–212. University
Park: Pennsylvania State University Press, 2004.

Noonan, John T., Jr. "Bribery in John of Salisbury." In *Proceedings of the VIIth International Congress of Medieval Canon Law, Cambridge, 23–27 July 1984*, 197–
203. Monumenta Iuris Canonici ser. C, Subsidia 8. Vatican City: Biblioteca
Apostolica Vaticana, 1988.

Olsen, Glenn W. "John of Salisbury's Humanism." In *Gli Unamesimi Medievali*, ed.
Claudio Leonardi, 447–68. Florence: SISMEL, Edizioni del Galluzzo, 1998.

Shibata, Heizaburo. *Chuusei no Haru: Sohrusuberi no Jon no Shisoh Sekai* [*Medieval
Spring: John of Salisbury's World of Ideas*]. Tokyo: Keio University Press,
2002.

Southern, R. W. *Scholastic Humanism and the Unification of Europe*, v. 1. Oxford: Blackwell, 1995.

Wilks, Michael, ed. *The World of John of Salisbury*. Studies in Church History Subsidia 3. Oxford: Basil Blackwell, 1984.

Works on the Writings of John of Salisbury: *Entheticus*

Hall, J. B. "Notes on the 'Entheticus' of John of Salisbury." *Traditio* 39 (1983): 444–47.

Nederman, Cary J., and Arlene Feldwick. "To the Court and Back Again: The Origins and Dating of the *Entheticus de Dogmate Philosophorum* of John of Salisbury." *Journal of Medieval and Renaissance Studies* 21 (1991): 129–45.

Pepin, Ronald E. "Fulgentius—The Enigmatic *Furvus* in John of Salisbury's 'Entheticus'." *Mittellateinisches Jahrbuch* 23 (1988): 119–25.

———. *Literature of Satire in the Twelfth Century: A Neglected Mediaeval Genre*. Lewiston, NY: The Edwin Mellen Press, 1988.

———. "John of Salisbury's *Entheticus* and the Classical Tradition of Satire." *Florilegium* 3 (1981): 215–27.

Works on the Writings of John of Salisbury: *Metalogicon*

Drew, Alison. "Language and Logic in John of Salisbury's *Metalogicon*." Ph.D. Dissertation, University of Cambridge, 1986.

Gerl, H.-B. "Zum mittelalterlichen Spannungsfeld von Logik, Dialektik und Rhetorik: Die Programmatik des *Metalogicon* von Johannes von Salisbury." *Studia mediewistyczne* 22 (1983): 37–51.

Godman, Peter. "*Opus consummatum, omnium artium . . . imago*: From Bernard of Chartres to John of Hauvilla." *Zeitschrift für Deutsches Altertum und Deutsche Literatur* 124 (1995): 26–71.

Goeglein, Tamara A. "The Problem of Monsters and Universals in 'The Owl and the Nightingale' and John of Salisbury's *Metalogicon*." *Journal of English and Germanic Philology* 94 (1995): 190–206

Hall, J. B. "Toward a Text of John of Salisbury's 'Metalogicon'." *Studi Medievali* 3rd ser., 24 (1983): 791–816.

Headley, Brian. "A New Look at John of Salisbury's Educational Theory." In *Knowledge and the Sciences in Medieval Philosophy: Proceedings of the Eighth International Congress of Medieval Philosophy (S.I.E.P.M.), Helsinki, 24–29 August 1987*, 3 vols., ed. Monika Asztalos, John E. Murdoch, and Ilkka Niiniluoto, v. 2, 502–11. Helsinki: Yliopistopaino, 1990.

Keats-Rohan, K. S. B. "The Chronology of John of Salisbury's Studies in France: A Reading of 'Metalogicon' II.10." *Studi Medievali* 3rd ser., 28 (1987): 193–203.

————. "The Textual Tradition of John of Salisbury's *Metalogicon*." *Revue d'Histoire des Textes* 16 (1986): 229–82.

Kühne, Udo. "*Nodus in scirpo—Enodatio quaestionis*: Eine Denkfigur bei Johannes von Salisbury und Alanus von Lille." *Antike und Abendland* 44 (1998): 163–76.

Nederman, Cary J. "Knowledge, Virtue, and the Path to Wisdom: The Unexamined Aristotelianism of John of Salisbury's *Metalogicon*." *Mediaeval Studies* 51 (1989): 268–86.

————. "Nature, Sin, and the Origins of Society: The Ciceronian Tradition in Medieval Political Thought." *Journal of the History of Ideas* 49 (1988): 3–26.

Seit, Stefan. "Die Orientierung des Denkens in der unvermeidlichkeit der Sprache: Johannes' von Salisbury *ratio indifferentiae*." In *Prudentia und Contemplatio: Ethik und Metaphysik im Mittelalter*, ed. Johannes Brachtendorf, 120–41. Paderborn: Ferdinand Schöningh, 2002.

Tacchella, Enrico. "Giovanni di Salisbury e i Cornificiani." *Sandalion* 3 (1980): 273–313.

Tobin, Rosemary Barton. "The Cornifician Motif in John of Salisbury's *Metalogicon*." *History of Education* 13 (1984): 1–6.

Trovato, Mario. "The Semantic Value of *Ingegno* and Dante's *Ulysses* in the Light of the *Metalogicon*." *Modern Philology* 84 (1987): 258–66.

Works on the Writings of John of Salisbury:
Policraticus

Canning, Joseph. *A History of Political Thought 300–1450*. London: Routledge, 1996.

Colish, Marcia L. "The Virtuous Pagan: Dante and the Christian Tradition." In *The Unbounded Community*, ed. William Caferro and Duncan G. Fisher, 43–91. New York: Garland Press, 1996.

De Rentis, Dina. "Für eine neue Geschichte der Nachahmungskategorie: *Imitatio morum* und *lectio auctorum* in *Policraticus* VII,10." In *Artes im Mittelalter*, ed. Ursula Schaefer, 161–73. Berlin: Akademie-Verlag, 1999.

Dutton, Paul Edward. "*Illustre Civitatis et Populi Exemplum*: Plato's *Timaeus* and the Transmission from Calcidius to the End of the Twelfth Century of a Tripartite Scheme of Society." *Mediaeval Studies* 45 (1983): 79–119.

Dyson, W.R. *Normative Theories of Society and Government in Five Medieval Thinkers: St. Augustine, John of Salisbury, Giles of Rome, St. Thomas Aquinas, and Marsilius of Pauda*. Lewiston, NY: Edwin Mellen Press, 2004.

Faci Lacasta, Javier. "El *Policraticus* de Juan de Salisbury y el mundo antiguo." In *Estudios dedicators al profesor D. Angel Ferrari Nuñez*, 2 vols., ed. M.A. Ladero Quesada, 2:343–62. Madrid: Universidad Complutense, 1984.

Forhan, Kate Langdon. "The Not-So-Divided Self: Reading Augustine in the Twelfth Century." *Augustiniana* 42 (1992): 95–110.

————. "Salisburian Stakes: The Uses of 'Tyranny' in John of Salisbury's *Policraticus*." *History of Political Thought* 11 (1990): 397–407.

———. "A Twelfth-Century 'Bureaucrat' and the Life of the Mind: John of Salisbury's *Policraticus.*" Ph.D. Dissertation, Department of Political Science, The Johns Hopkins University, 1987.

———. "A Twelfth-Century 'Bureaucrat' and the Life of the Mind: The Political Thought of John of Salisbury." *Proceedings of the PMR Conference* 10 (1985): 65–74.

Keats-Rohan, K. S. B. "Marklandus in 'Policraticum' Ioannis Saresberiensis." *Studi Medievali* 3rd ser., 1 (1988): 375–421.

Ladero Quesada, Miguel Ángel. "El emperador Trajano como modelo de príncipes en la Edad Media: el príncipe en *Policraticus.*" *Anuario de estudios medievales* 29 (1999): 501–25.

Lee, Hee-Man. "A Study on the Theory of the Tyrant of John of Salisbury" [in Korean]. *Soongsilsahak* 11 (1998): 221–57

———. "The Theory of Kingship of John of Salisbury" [in Korean]. *Soyangchungsesayongu* 2 (1997): 1–29.

———. "John of Salisbury and the *Policraticus*" [in Korean]. *Soongsilsahak* 9 (1996): 261–90.

Monahan, Arthur P. *Consent, Coercion, and Limit: The Medieval Origins of Parliamentary Democracy.* Montrèal and Kingston: McGill-Queen's University Press, 1987.

Moos, Peter von. *Geschichte als Topik: Das rhetorische Exemplum von der Antike zur Neuzeit und die* historiae *im "Politicraticus" Johanns von Salisbury.* Studien zur Lituratur und Gesellschaft des Mittelalters und der frühen Neuzeit 2. Hildesheim: Georg Olms Verlag, 1988 (1st ed.), 1996 (2nd ed.).

Nederman, Cary J. "The Origins of 'Policy': Fiscal Administration and Economic Principles in Later Twelfth-Century England." In *Rhetoric and Renewal in the Latin West 1100–1500: Essays Presented to John O. Ward*, ed. Constant J. Mews, Cary J. Nederman, and Rodney Thomson, 149–68. Turnhout, Belgium: Brepols, 2003.

———. "Social Bodies and the Non-Christian 'Other' in the Twelfth Century: John of Salisbury and Peter of Celle." In *Meeting the Foreign in the Middle Ages*, ed. Albrecht Classen, 192–201. New York/London: Routledge, 2002.

———. "The Virtues of Necessity: John of Salisbury's Economic Thought." *Viator* 33 (2002): 54–68.

———. "Mechanics and Citizens: The Reception of the Aristotelian Idea of Citizenship in Late Medieval Europe." *Vivarium* 40 (July 2002): 75–102.

———. "Liberty, Community, and Toleration: Freedom and Function in Medieval Political Thought." In *Difference and Dissent: Theories of Toleration in Medieval and Early Modern Europe*, ed. Cary J. Nederman and John Christian Laursen, 17–37. Lanham, MD: Rowman & Littlefield, 1996.

———. "The Meaning of 'Aristotelianism' in Medieval Moral and Political Thought." *Journal of the History of Ideas* 57 (1996): 563–85.

———. "Aristotelianism and the Origins of 'Political Science' in the Twelfth Century." *Journal of the History of Ideas* 52 (1991): 179–94.

———. "A Duty to Kill: John of Salisbury's Theory of Tyrannicide." *Review of Politics* 50 (1988): 365–89.

————. "The Physiological Significance of the Organic Metaphor in John of Salisbury's *Policraticus.*" *History of Political Thought* 8 (1987): 211–23.

————. "The Aristotelian Doctrine of the Mean and John of Salisbury's Concept of Liberty." *Vivarium* 24 (1986): 128–42.

———— and John Brückmann. "Aristotelianism in John of Salisbury's *Policraticus.*" *Journal of the History of Philosophy* 21 (1983): 203–29.

———— and Catherine Campbell. "Priests, Kings, and Tyrants: Spiritual and Temporal Power in John of Salisbury's *Policraticus.*" *Speculum* 66 (1991): 572–90.

———— and N. Elaine Lawson. "The Frivolities of Courtiers Follow the Footprints of Women: Public Women and the Crisis of Virility in John of Salisbury." In *Ambiguous Realities: Women in the Middle Ages and Renaissance*, ed. Carole Levin and Jeanie Watson, 82–96. Detroit: Wayne State University Press, 1987.

———— and Jacqui True. "The Third Sex: The Idea of the Hermaphrodite in the Twelfth Century." *Journal of the History of Sexuality* 6 (1996): 497–517.

Pepin, Ronald E. "Master John's Hilarity." *Hatcher Review* 2 (1985): 399–403.

Rowlstone, Peter. "John of Salisbury and the Theory of Tyranny: The Practical Application of Abstract Ideas in the Twelfth Century." M.A. Thesis, Medieval Studies Program, University of Bristol, 2001.

Rollo, David. *Glamorous Sorcery: Magic and Literacy in the High Middle Ages.* Minneapolis: University of Minnesota Press, 2000.

Van Laarhoven, Jan. "Titles and Subtitles of the *Policraticus*: A Proposal." *Vivarium* 32 (1994): 131–60.

Works on the Writings of John of Salisbury: *Historia Pontificalis*

Brooke, Christopher. "Aspects of John of Salisbury's *Historia Pontificalis.*" In *Intellectual Life in the Middle Ages: Essays Presented to Margaret Gibson*, ed. Lesley Smith and Benedicta Ward, 185–95. London: The Hambleton Press, 1992.

Ray, Roger. "Rhetorical Skepticism and Verisimilar Narrative in John of Salisbury's *Historia Pontificalis.*" In *Classical Rhetoric and Medieval Historiography*, ed. Ernst Breisach, 61–102. Studies in Medieval Culture 19. Kalamazoo: The Medieval Institute, 1985.

Ward, John O. "Some Principles of Rhetorical Historiography in the Twelfth Century." In *Classical Rhetoric and Medieval Historiography*, ed. Ernst Breisach, 103–65. Studies in Medieval Culture 19. Kalamazoo: The Medieval Institute, 1985.

Works on the Writings of John of Salisbury: Miscellaneous

Hirata, Yoko. "St. Anselm and Two Clerks of Thomas Becket." In *Anselm: Aosta, Bec and Canterbury*, ed. D. E. Luscombe and G. R. Evans, 323–33. Sheffield: Sheffield Academic Press, 1996.

————. "John of Salisbury and his Correspondents: A Study of the Epistolary Relationships between John of Salisbury and his Correspondents." Ph.D. Dissertation, University of Sheffield, 1991.

Löfstedt, Bengt. "Notizen zu den Briefen des Johannes von Salisbury." *Acta Classica* 30 (1987): 75–80.

Nadeau, Alain. "Notes on the Significance of John of Salisbury's *Vita Anselmi*." In *Twenty-Five Years (1969–1994) of Anselm Studies*, ed. Frederic van Fleteren and Joseph C. Schnaubelt, 1–27. Lewiston, NY: Edwin Mellen Press, 1996.

Nederman, Cary J. "Aristotelian Ethics and John of Salisbury's *Letters*." *Viator* 18 (1987): 161–73.

Works on the Influence of John of Salisbury

Forhan, Kate Langdon. "Polycracy, Obligation, and Revolt: The Body Politic in John of Salisbury and Christine de Pizan." In *Politics, Gender, and Genre: The Political Thought of Christine de Pizan*, ed. Margaret Brabant, 33–52. Boulder, CO: Westview Press, 1992.

Hicks, Eric. "A Mirror for Misogynists: John of Salisbury's *Policraticus* (8.11) in the Translation of Denis Foulechat (1372)." In *Reinterpreting Christine de Pizan*, ed. Earl Jeffrey Richards, 77–107. Athens: University of Georgia Press, 1992.

McHam, Sarah Blake. "Donatello's Bronze *David* and *Judith* as Metaphors of Medici Rule in Florence." *Art Bulletin* 83 (2001): 32–47.

Web Sites Related to John of Salisbury

http://perso.magic.fr/relet/StLoup/Les_Protagonistes/Jean_de_Salisbury/JEAN_DE_SAL ISBURY.htm

http://www.bautz.de/bbkl/j/Johannes_v_sali.shtml

http://www.baylor.edu/~Kristi_Klick/

INDEX

Note: Following standard practice, all medieval figures are listed alphabetically by their given Christian names, even if their surname is known.